HELP!

I WOKE UP

A SENIOR CITIZEN

AND

DON'T KNOW WHAT TO DO

An Information and Reference Guide for Everyone

"Help I Woke Up a Senior Citizen, and
Don't Know What to Do"
To order this book via
The Author: 1-248 358-5165
E-mail: franksinger@peoplepc.com

1st Books - Internet: www.1stbooks.com
Toll-free: 1-800 839-8640
Specify Book # ISBN - 1-58820-569X

HELP!

I WOKE UP

A SENIOR CITIZEN

AND

DON'T KNOW WHAT TO DO

An Information and Reference Guide for Everyone

By

Frank Singer

Copyright © 2000 by Frank Singer

All rights reserved.
No part of this book may be reproduced, restored in a retrieval system, or transmitted by means, electronic, mechanical, photocopying, recording, or otherwise, without written consent from the author.

ISBN: 1-58820-569-X

S0S PUBLICATIONS, BIRMINGHAM, MICHIGAN

1stBooks - rev. 11/15/00

ACKNOWLEDGMENTS

AARP...Alzheimer's Association...American Cancer Association...American Diabetes Association...American Dental Association...American Dietetic Association...American Heart Association...Area Agency on Aging, Region 1-B, Michigan...Arthritis Foundation... Health Care Financing Administration...U.S. Dep't of Health & Human Services... National Institute on Aging...National Eye Institute... National Institute of Health...National Health Information Center...Consumer Information Center...Centers for Disease Control...American Medical Association...Blue Cross/Blue Shield, Michigan...Citizens for Better Care, Michigan...Commission on Senior Affairs, Southfield, Michigan...Social Security Administration...Michigan State Office of Services to the Aging...Pension Benefit Guarantee Corporation...Michigan Oakland County Health Department...U.S. Department of State.

Drs. George Dean, Howard Schwartz, Larry Lipnick, Family Practitioners...Dr. Isaac Grinberg, Cardiologist...Dr. Jack Kartush, Otolaryngologist...Dr. Tim Kosinski, DDS... Scott Friedman, Dermatologist & Cosmetic Surgeon...Darlene Sowa, Exercise Physiologist...James Schuster, Elder Law Attorney.

And, of course, I can't forget my family's contributions. My wife Helen, who would not put up with my procrastinating, who helped with the proofreading, and checking sources, and my sons Robert and Steven who read, encouraged, and kept telling me to stop adding and revising, and finish with what I had. Love you, Family.
To everyone else, my deepest thanks and appreciation.

PREFACE

You wake up one day, and lo and behold, you realize you are eligible for Social Security, or Medicare, or both. What to do? When to do it? What does the future hold?

All you know is that the old bones creak, and you *"ain't what you used to be"*. Questions, questions! Where can I find out about senior housing options, or places to retire? My spouse is an invalid. Where can I find out about caregivers? What about healthcare? Benefits? Is it safe to exercise or exert yourself?

These and a host of other problems that confront us in our "Golden Age" can be frightening, confusing. How do we cope? How, when and where do we find answers, counsel, references.

At the same time, while there are problems, there are also positives - the opportunities to enhance the enjoyment and quality of our lives. So we have included information on aging successfully, information on special discounts and services for Seniors, tips on travel and vacations, nutrition and fitness guidelines, and more. These days, retiring doesn't mean retiring from life. It means doing the things you couldn't or wouldn't do beforehand.

That is the purpose of this book. To provide you with both the information you need to handle the important situations that crop up before, or during, your aging years, as well as as how to enjoy them.

FOREWORD

One day, my wife asked me what was the second best thing that ever happened to me. My answer surprised her because I said, *"My stroke!"*. Let me explain.

The year I turned 65, I suffered a stroke; actually a series of strokes. T.I.A.'s (trans-ischemic attacks) they called them, because they came and went. I was hospitalized several times. It was a very frightening period, especially during the episodes of paralysis. I thought surely that my days were numbered, or that I would end up a hopeless invalid, a fate I dreaded worse than death, and still do. Fortunately, with the help and guidance of my good doctors, I pulled through without permanent damage.

Several things resulted from the whole experience. For one, I retired from business. Next, it forced me to face up to my mortality. What would I do with the rest of my life? How would I do it?

Again, fortune was on my side. My doctors recommended a radical change in my diet, plus an excercise regimen. The diet was low fat, low cholesterol, low salt, based on "Pritikin". I followed it religiously. The exercise was aerobic walking. In 6 months, I shed 18 unneeded pounds. Within a year, I felt better, physically, than when I was 50.

The other good thing that happened during my R & R, was discovering "Community Access". This is television produced by residents of the community, and broadcast on the city's cable channel. I took the free TV courses offered - got involved, worked as a crew member, produced my own programs, and eventually was offered a part-time job with the city. I've been at it ever since.

I still occasionally get hit with a T.I.A., and developed other conditions that come with the aging process. But, I have learned to cope. I know I'm not going to get out of this world alive. Until then, Lord willing, I'll continue to work at being mentally stimulated and physically active.

For me, life **began anew** at 65. That's why I said at the beginning - my stroke was one of the best things that ever happened to me.

- **Frank Singer**

INTRODUCTION

This book is for - *Active Agers...Sedentary Seniors...Children of Aging Parents...the Disabled...the Homebound...Baby Boomers...Caretakers* - and anyone interested in geriatrics...anyone interested in living long enough to become a Senior, and to the Businesses and Service Providers catering to the Seniors.

You will find in this book things you didn't even know you didn't know (or possibly care to). You will learn where to go for information, reference, guidance or counsel, when the need arises.

Subject matter has been written as concisely as we could make it ("just the facts Ma'am").

Interspersed throughout, you will find some humor (we hope), homilies and trivia. Included, too, are inspirational notes about famous and not-so-famous Seniors, all of which is designed to make this, not just a reference, but also an enjoyable read.

Information in this book comes, largely, from Government and Government-funded Agencies...Social and Non-Profit Agencies, organizations such as the American Association of Retired Persons... Medical Associations.... Newspapers, Magazines and Periodicals targeting Seniors.... and Library References. I did the work so you wouldn't have to.

It would be impossible to list all the people whose brains I picked in the course of putting this together. However, there are a few whom I would like to thank in particular - Joyce Hunt, Senior Affairs Advisor, Area Agency on Aging Region 1-B, Michigan... Dorothy Szuba, Librarian II-Adult, City of Southfield, Michigan ...O'Brien Robertson, Social Security Administration, Pontiac, Michigan ....Lynn Robertson, Public Relations, Blue Cross/Blue Shield Michigan.... to the doctors, and other individuals who contributed their knowledge and expertise. To all who made this book possible, I am deeply grateful.

TABLE OF CONTENTS

1. **SOCIAL SECURITY – SOCIAL IT AIN'T – GIMME SECURITY** 1

    - Eligibility
    - Spouses Benefits
    - Divorcee Benefit
    - Other Family Member Benefits

    Supplemental Security Income (SSI) for Those in Financial Need

    - for Citizens
    - for Non-Citizens

    Information Please:

    - Current Changes in the Law
    - Pro's and Cons of Taking Early Benefits at Age 62
    - Work After 65? Effect on Benefits
    - Status Changes You Must Report to **S. S.**

2. **MEDICARE – GOTTA HAVE IT** 7

    - Eligibility
    - Part A – Covers Hospital Costs – Pay No Premiums
    - Part B – Covers Doctors Visits, et al – Pay Premiums
    - What Medicare Pays
    - What Medicare Does **Not** Pay
    - Special Services Now Covered

3. **BUYING MEDIGAP (SUPPLEMENTAL) INSURANCE** 17

    - What Is It
    - The 10 Standardized Plans
    - Insurance Information Sources

4. **HEALTH CARE'S LAST RESORT BUT YOU SHOULDN'T KNOW FROM IT** 23

    - How Medicaid Differs from Medicare
    - Eligibility Requirements

- Resources at Risk
- What They Can't Take Away from You

5. **HMO'S – MANAGED CARE – GOOD OR BAD FOR YOU?** 27
    - What Is It
    - How It Works
    - Pros & Cons
    - Types of Plans
    - How to Enroll
    - How to Dis-enroll

6. **LONG TERM CARE – SOMETHING TO CARE ABOUT** 33
    - Custodial Versus Skilled Nursing Home Care
    - Alternatives to Nursing Home Care
    - Finding Caregivers
    - Insurance Plans

7. **HOSPICE CARE FOR THE TERMINALLY ILL IT'S A BUMMER NO MATTER WHAT** 45
    - What Is It
    - When Applicable
    - Care Options

8. **BLAME IT ON OLD AGE** 49
    - Your Aging Eyes
    - Your Aging Hearing
    - Your Aging Skin
    - Your Aging Teeth

9. *"WHY ME"* **ILLNESSES** 65
    - Breast Cancer
    - Prostate Cancer
    - Heart Disease
    - Stroke
    - High Blood Pressure
    - Diabetes
    - Alzheimer's Disease

10. HOUSING 83

- Assisted Living
- Continuing Care Retirement Communities (CCRC)
- Continuum of Care Residences (CCR)
- Independent Housing
- Nursing Homes
- Respite Care
- Shared Housing
- Subsidized Housing

11. PENSION PLANS - WHERE'S THE MONEY? 87

- Protection Under the Law
- Types of Plans
- Common Problems & Questions
- Sources of Help
- Other Sources of Help
- Legal Service Programs

12. HEALTH AND FITNESS – GO FOR IT 93

- You're Never Too Old
- Programs for the Fit, Frail, & Elderly
- Nutrition & Exercise Go Hand In Hand
    a. Nutrition Pyramid
    b. Activity Pyramid

13. HITTING THE ROAD - TRAVEL FOR SENIORS 105

- Deals, Discounts
- Traveling Abroad, Things to Know
- Travel Agencies for Disabled
- Special Vacations

14 ELDER LAW 113

- Legal Assistance Programs
- Wills, Trusts
- Living Wills
- Power of Attorney

15. APPENDIX 119

- Primary Information Sources
- Toll-Free Numbers
- The Internet
- Medicare Resources Directories
- State Insurance Departments Directory
- 2000 Changes in Social Security, Medicare, SSI
- Medicare Changes in the Year 2000

CHAPTER 1

SOCIAL SECURITY

"When I was young, I used to think that money was the most important thing in the world. Now that I am old, I know it is!"
                                                                                -Oscar Wilde

How right you are, Oscar. Ask any one living on Social Security, and very little else. It is an economic and emotional lifeline for the millions who depend on it. Rest assured that despite all the Congressional debate and posturing about what to do about Social Security, it "ain't" going away. It's the one issue that unites all current beneficiaries and those who expect to live long enough to collect social security. Changes may be made, but the basic philosophy and need for it, remains. Meanwhile, here is some basic information you need to know.

Getting Social Security is **not** automatic. You **must** apply!

Applicants are urged to apply at least 3 months before becoming eligible for benefits, at which time the Agency reviews the exact requirements for entitlement.

You can receive benefits at age 62, 63, 64, or 65. But weigh that decision carefully. We're living longer. With inflation and rising health costs, we need more money as the years go by. When my wife elected to apply for benefits at age 62, we were swayed by the three additional years she would receive benefits. Three years later, we could have used that higher benefit. Consider-

At age 62 - benefits are reduced 20 %!
　　　　63 -　　　"　　　"　　　"　　13-1/2 %
　　　　64 -　　　"　　　"　　　"　　6-2/3 %

So, unless you have a big nest egg or a substantial pension to fall back on, hold out for age 65, if you can. Another thing to think about. The age for retirement will be extended to 67, and applies right now for those born in 1960 or after.

To help you decide when to apply, request **Form SSA-7004-SM**

"Personal Earnings & Benefits Statement".

In addition to the retired worker, benefits may also apply to: -

- A Spouse
- A Divorced Spouse
- Independently Divorced Spouse
- Child or Disabled Child/Adult Child
- Aged Widow(er)
- Surviving Divorced Spouse
- Disabled Widow(er)
- Mother & Father
- Parent
- Lump Sum Death Payment

If you fit any of these categories, you **must apply** to receive benefits, or to learn if you are eligible for them.

The rules and requirements are too lengthy to cover here. Phone numbers and a list of helpful publications available from S.S. are found at the end of this chapter.

* * *

SUPPLEMENTAL SECURITY INCOME

S.S.I. is a program for low income seniors, the disabled or children who are disabled. Although run by the Social Security Administration, its monies do not come from Social Security funds, but rather from the general revenues of the U. S. Treasury. Most people who get SSI can also get food stamps and "Medicaid" assistance.

As with Social Security, you **must apply** and you must meet certain requirements. Some of these are-

- age 65 or older
- U.S. citizen, or legal resident
- blind or disabled
- limited income or assets

HOW MUCH MONEY CAN YOU GET

That depends on the following factors:

Your Income and Assets

The basic monthly S.S.I. payment is the same in all States. The maximum benefit, for the year 2000, is $512 for one person, $769 for a Couple. For Assets, maximum is $2,000 for an Individual, and $3,000 a Couple.

Where you live

Some states add money to the basic rate. So depending upon where you live, you might get more than the basic rate. But, you will get less if you have other income, or are getting some support for food and shelter.

* * *

As with Social Security, the SSI program has special plans to help the disabled who want to try to work without suddenly losing their benefits, or Medicaid coverage.

* * *

REPORT ALL STATUS CHANGES

It's important that you **report these changes** in status to Social Security, as they can affect your benefits and/or family members:

- Change in Estimated Earnings
- Address Change
- Unable to Manage Your Funds

- Receiving a Pension from "Non-covered" Work
- Change in Marital Status
- Name Change

- Caring for a Child Receiving Benefits
- Adoption of a Child
- Change Direct Deposit
- A Beneficiary is Convicted of a Crime
- If You Leave the U. S. A.
- Death of a Beneficiary

* * *

FOR INFORMATION & PUBLICATIONS

SOCIAL SECURITY'S TOLL-FREE NUMBER IS-

1-800-772-1213

Call 24 hours a day, 7 days a week, including holidays, but be prepared for busy, busy signals. To speak to a human being, instead of those automated voice instructions to "push this button" etc, call between 7 A. M. and 7 P. M. weekdays.

FOR THE DEAF, OR HARD OF HEARING
Call The "TTY" Number

1-800 -325 - 0778, WEEKDAYS

* * *

Food for Thought

There is no age limit to creativity!

Grandma Moses started painting at age 76

George Bernard Shaw was still writing plays at 93

Benjamin Franklin helped write the Constitution at 81

Remember!

"It's not the number of years in your life that counts, it's the life in your years!"

FREE PUBLICATIONS

#05-10035	-	*Retirement* - a guide to benefits
#05-10077	-	*What You Need to Know When You Get Retirement or Survivors Benefits*
#05-10069	-	*How Work Affects Your SS Benefits*
#05-10038	-	*When You Retire From Your Own Business: What SS Needs to Know*
#05-10100	-	*Food Stamps & Other Nutrition Programs*
#05- 10101	-	*Food Stamp Facts*
#05-10084	-	*Survivors Benefits*

#05-11000	-	*(SSI) Supplemental Security Program*
#05-10029	-	*Disability*
#05-10026	-	*SS and SSI Benefits for Children With Disabilities*
#05-10095	-	*Working While Disabled: How SS Can Help*
#05-10052	-	*If You Are Blind: How SS & SSI Can Help*

For Women - Divorced, Widowed or Other, ask for the booklet-

"Social Security, What Every Woman Should Know"

Other special publications are also available including how to get representation, or appealing a decision concerning benefits or eligiblity. Call or visit your local Social Security Office for a personal interview, or for information in general.

CHAPTER 2

MEDICARE

"Now that we have Medicare, we can enjoy diseases we once couldn't afford".

Yes, despite the aches and pains, heaped upon us in our advancing years, they still beat the alternative. To help beat the "alternative", there is Medicare.

Like Social Security, changes will be made to keep it solvent in the future. But it will still be your medical "safety net".

WHAT IS MEDICARE?

A Federal Health Insurance Program for people age 65 or older, and certain disabled persons.

IS EVERY ONE ENTITLED TO MEDICARE?

NO!

You or your Spouse must have earned enough working credits to receive Social Security

IS ENROLLMENT AUTOMATIC?

YES - If you are already collecting Social Security

NO - If you are **not** collecting Social Security, you **must** file when you reach 65, or government employment is involved, or if you have kidney disease.

To Learn if You Are Eligible:

- Under Social Security
- Under Railroad Retirement System
- Under a Government Plan

visit your local Social Security Office, or call -

1-800-772-1213

and while you're at it, ask for your -

"Medicare Handbook"

It contains the answers to most of your questions.

* * *

About Your Card

If you are already receiving Social Security or Railroad Retirement benefits, you will automatically receive a Medicare card when you reach age 65. Follow the card instructions on whether or not you wish to enroll in Part B.

- **Always keep your Medicare Card handy.**

- **Always carry it with you when away from home, or when traveling.**

* * *

THE TWO PARTS OF MEDICARE

PART "A" - HOSPITAL INSURANCE - NO PREMIUMS

Covers Hospital, Skilled Care Nursing Facility, Home Health, and Hospice Care

PART "B" - MEDICAL INSURANCE - PAY PREMIUMS

Covers Doctor Visits, Outpatient Hospital Services, some Medical Equipment, and supplies and services not covered by Part "A"

Enrollment in Part "B" is voluntary
Premiums are deducted from your monthly Social Security, Railroad Retirement, or Civil Service Retirement check.

Both Plans have **"Deductibles"** and **"Co-Insurance"** features.

DEDUCTIBLES
The amount **you** have to pay before Medicare pays

The "Deductibles" vary for each Plan. However, once you have reached the deductible level for that Calendar Year, you pay no more for that year.

CO-INSURANCE

Means you **share** the cost with Medicare.

Again, the costs vary with each Plan. For example, on Part "B", currently, Medicare pays only 80 % of the costs. You pay the other 20 %. That is why it may be advisable to get what is called **"Medigap"** or supplemental insurance to cover your otherwise out-of-pocket expenses. (See Chapter 3 for more details on Medigap)

* * *

ARE THE SERVICES OF ALL KINDS OF MEDICAL PROFESSIONALS COVERED?

Services must be provided by a doctor of medicine or of osteopathy. Some exceptions may be made in the case of chiropractors, podiatrists, psychologists, nurses, and others who may be considered medical professionals, but not doctors. However, the exceptions are very restrictive. If in doubt, check with the service provider, and with your Medicare carrier.

Medicare may also pay for care in special approved health care facilities such as Rural Health Clinics, Community Mental Health Centers, and Certified Medical Laboratories. Again, check beforehand to make sure you will be covered.

AREA OF COVERAGE

Your health care is covered in the 50 States and certain U.S. territories such as Puerto Rico and Guam. Some exceptions may be made for Canada and Mexico, if in an emergency, a U.S. hospital is not as close as the other country's hospital.

In any event, when traveling outside the country, it is wise to take out travel medical coverage. Some Medigap policies may cover you. Check your supplemental insurance policy before you go on a trip.

* * *

AID PROGRAMS FOR LOW-INCOME BENEFICIARIES

Medicare beneficiaries with low incomes and few assets may qualify for state assistance in paying for health care costs.

You may also be eligible if you are elderly and poor, or disabled and poor, and eligible for Medicare. Two programs offer help:

(QMB) QUALIFIED MEDICARE BENEFICIARY

Pays premiums, deductibles, and co-insurance.

To qualify, your income must be at, or below, the specified national poverty level. Assets, too, cannot exceed current levels. (See chart in Appendix for "Changes in Social Security, Medicare, and SSI for the Year 2000"

(SLMB) SPECIFIED LOW-INCOME MEDICARE BENEFICIARY

Pays only for Part "B" premiums.

You must be eligible for Part "A".

Income slightly higher than the national poverty level, and have limited assets.

Since the funds for these two programs are administered through the State, you must file an application for **Medicaid**.

To find out if you are eligible, and how to apply, contact the -

**local Area Agency on Aging,
or
the State or local Medicaid office.**

Or, you can get the phone number of the nearest medical assistance office in your State or County, by calling, toll-free -

1-800-638-6833

* * *

YOUR MEDICARE BENEFITS

Medicare Part A (Hospital Insurance) Covers:	What You Pay in 1999* in the Original Medicare Plan
Hospital Stays: Semiprivate room, meals, general nursing and other hospital services and supplies. This does not include private duty nursing, a television or telephone in your room, or a private room, unless medically necessary. Inpatient mental health care coverage in a psychiatric facility is limited to 190 days in a lifetime.	For each benefit period you pay: • A total of $768 for a hospital stay of 1-60 days. • $192 per day for days 61-90 of a hospital stay. • $384 per day for days 91-150 of a hospital stay. • All costs for each day beyond 150 days.
Skilled Nursing Facility (SNF) Care:** Semi-private room, meals, skilled nursing and rehabilitative services, and other services and supplies (after a 3-day hospital stay).	For each benefit period you pay: • Nothing for the first 20 days. • Up to $96 per day for days 21-100. • All costs beyond the 100th day in the benefit period. If you have questions about SNF care and conditions of coverage, call your Fiscal Intermediary. This is the company that pays Medicare Part A bills
Home Health Care:** Part-time skilled nursing care, physical therapy, speech-language therapy, home health aide services, durable medical equipment (such as wheelchairs, hospital beds, oxygen, and walkers) and supplies, and other services	You pay: • Nothing for home health care services. • 20% of approved amount for durable medical equipment. If you have questions about home health care and conditions of coverage, call your Regional Home Health Intermediary
Hospice Care:** Medical and support services from a Medicare-approved hospice, drugs for symptom control and pain relief, short-term respite care, care in a hospice facility, hospital, or nursing home when necessary, and other services not otherwise covered by Medicare. Home care is also covered.	You pay: • A copayment of up to $5 for outpatient prescription drugs and a $5 per day copayment for inpatient respite care (short-term care given to a hospice patient by another care giver, so that the usual care giver can rest). The copayment can change depending on where you live. If you have questions about hospice care and conditions of coverage, call your Regional Home Health Intermediary
Blood: Given at a hospital or skilled nursing facility during a covered stay.	You pay: • For the first 3 pints of blood.

* New Part A and B amounts will be available by January 1, 2000.
** You must meet certain conditions in order for Medicare to cover these services.

If you have general questions about Medicare Part A, call your Fiscal Intermediary. This is the company that pays Medicare Part A bills

Medicare & You 2000

YOUR MEDICARE BENEFITS

Medicare Part B (Medical Insurance) Covers:	What You Pay in 1999* in the Original Medicare Plan
Medical and Other Services: Doctors' services (except for routine physical exams), outpatient medical and surgical services and supplies, diagnostic tests, ambulatory surgery center facility fees for approved procedures, and durable medical equipment (such as wheelchairs, hospital beds, oxygen, and walkers). Also covers outpatient physical and occupational therapy including speech-language therapy, and mental health services.	**You pay:** • $100 deductible (pay once per calendar year). • 20% of approved amount after the deductible, except in the outpatient setting. • 20% of $1,500 for all outpatient physical and speech therapy services and 20% of $1,500 for all outpatient occupational therapy services. You pay all charges above $1,500. **(Hospital outpatient therapy services do not count towards the $1,500 limits.)** • 50% for most outpatient mental health.
Clinical Laboratory Service: Blood tests, urinalysis, and more.	**You pay:** • Nothing for services.
Home Health Care:** Part-time skilled care, home health aide services, durable medical equipment when supplied by a home health agency while getting Medicare covered home health care, and other supplies and services.	**You pay:** • Nothing for services. • 20% of approved amount for durable medical equipment.
Outpatient Hospital Services: Services for the diagnosis or treatment of an illness or injury.	**You pay:** • 20% of the charged amount (after the deductible). During the year 2000, this will change to a set copayment amount.
Blood: Pints of blood needed as an outpatient, or as part of a Part B covered service.	**You pay:** • For the first 3 pints of blood, then 20% of the approved amount for additional pints of blood (after the deductible).

* New Part A & B amounts will be available by January 1, 2000.
** You must meet certain conditions in order for Medicare to cover these services.

Note: Actual amounts you must pay are higher if the doctor does not accept assignment If you have general questions about your Medicare Part B coverage, call your Medicare Carrier. This is the company that pays Medicare Part B bills

Medicare & You 2000

YOUR MEDICARE BENEFITS

Medicare Part B Covered Preventive Services	Who is covered...	What you pay...
Bone Mass Measurements: Varies with your health status.	Certain people with Medicare who are at risk for losing bone mass.	20% of the Medicare approved amount after the yearly Part B deductible.
Colorectal Cancer Screening: • Fecal Occult Blood Test - Once every year. • Flexible Sigmoidoscopy - Once every four years. • Colonoscopy - Once every two years if you are high risk for cancer of the colon. • Barium Enema - Doctor can substitute for sigmoidoscopy or colonoscopy.	All people with Medicare age 50 and older. However, there is no age limit for having a colonoscopy.	No coinsurance and no Part B deductible for the fecal occult blood test. For all other tests, 20% of the Medicare approved amount after the yearly Part B deductible.
Diabetes Monitoring: Includes coverage for glucose monitors, test strips, lancets, and self-management training.	All people with Medicare who have diabetes (insulin users and non-users).	20% of the Medicare approved amount after the yearly Part B deductible.
Mammogram Screening: Once every year.	All women with Medicare age 40 and older.	20% of the Medicare approved amount with no Part B deductible.
Pap Smear and Pelvic Examination: (Includes a clinical breast exam) Once every three years. Once every year if you are high risk for cervical or vaginal cancer, or if you are of childbearing age and have had an abnormal Pap smear in the preceding three years.	All women with Medicare.	No coinsurance and no Part B deductible for the Pap smear (clinical laboratory charge). For doctor services and all other exams, 20% of the Medicare approved amount with no Part B deductible.
Prostate Cancer Screening: Starting January 1, 2000 • Digital Rectal Examination - Once every year. • Prostate Specific Antigen (PSA) Test - Once every year.	All men with Medicare age 50 and older.	Generally, 20% of the Medicare approved amount after the yearly Part B deductible. No coinsurance and no Part B deductible for the PSA Test.
Vaccinations: • Flu Shot - Once every year. • Pneumonia Shot - One may be all you ever need, ask your doctor. • Hepatitis B Shot - If you are at medium to high risk for hepatitis.	All people with Medicare.	No coinsurance and no Part B deductible for flu and pneumonia shots if the doctor accepts assignment (see page 47). For Hepatitis B shots, 20% of the Medicare approved amount after the Part B deductible.

Medicare & You 2000

YOUR MEDICARE BENEFITS

Part B also helps pay for:

- Ambulance services (limited coverage).
- Artificial limbs and eyes.
- Braces - arm, leg, back, and neck.
- Chiropractic services (limited).
- Emergency care.
- Eyeglasses - one pair after cataract surgery with an intraocular lens.
- Kidney dialysis and kidney transplants.
- Medical supplies - items such as ostomy bags, surgical dressings, splints, casts, and some diabetic supplies.
- Outpatient prescription drugs (very limited).
- Preventive services
- Prosthetic devices, including breast prothesis after mastectomy.
- Services of practitioners such as clinical psychologists, and social workers, and nurse practitioners.
- Transplants - heart, lung, and liver (under certain conditions).
- X-rays and some other diagnostic tests.

What is not paid for by Medicare Part A and Part B in the Original Medicare Plan?

The Original Medicare Plan does not cover everything. Your out-of-pocket costs for health care will include but are not limited to:

- Your monthly Part B premium ($45.50 in 1999*).
- Deductibles, coinsurance or copayments when you get health care services (see the "What You Pay" part of the charts
- Outpatient prescription drugs (with only a few exceptions).
- Routine or yearly physical exams.
- Vaccinations except as listed
- Orthopedic shoes.
- Custodial care (help with bathing, dressing, toileting, and eating) at home or in a nursing home.
- Most dental care and dentures.
- Routine foot care.
- Hearing aids.
- Routine eye care.
- Health care you get while traveling outside of the United States (except under limited circumstances).
- Cosmetic surgery.

Outpatient physical and occupational therapy services, including speech-language therapy except for those you get in hospital outpatient departments, have limits for each calendar year. The Original Medicare Plan does pay for some preventive care, but not all of it

You may be able to get help to cover the costs Medicare does not cover   You may be able to join a Medicare managed care plan and get extra benefits

* New Part A and B amounts will be available by January 1, 2000.

Medicare & You 2000

―― FOR MORE INFORMATION ――

Free Medicare and Related Publications

To ask for a copy of...

- *Does Your Doctor or Supplier Accept Assignment?*
- *Guide to Choosing a Nursing Home*
- *Guide to Health Insurance for People With Medicare*
- *Health Plan Comparison Information*
- *Learning About Medicare Health Plans*
- *Medicare Coverage of Kidney Dialysis and Kidney Transplant Services*
- *Medicare Health Plan Quality and Satisfaction Information*
- *Medicare Home Health Care Services*
- *Medicare Hospice Benefits*
- *Medicare Preventive Services*
- *Medicare Supplemental Insurance (Medigap) Policies and Protections*
- *Medicare & You (Available in English, Spanish, Audio-tape, or Braille)*
- *Worksheet for Comparing Medicare Health Plans*
- *Your Guide to Medicare Medical Savings Accounts*
- *Your Guide to Private Fee-for-Service Plans*

Call: 1-800-MEDICARE (1-800-633-4227, TTY/TDD: 1-877-486-2048 for the hearing and speech impaired).

To request a copy of...

- *A Shopper's Guide to Long-term Care Insurance*

Write to:

NAIC
Publications Dept.,
120 West 12th Street
Suite 1100
Kansas City, MO 64105

Medicare & You 2000

CHAPTER 3

- MEDIGAP INSURANCE -
WITHOUT IT, OUT-OF-POCKET COSTS COULD BE UNHEALTHY

You know you're growing old when your address book is filled with names beginning with - "Doctor"

* * *

Medicare does not pay fully for all your healthcare costs.

Medigap Insurance policies are specifically designed to help pay for health care expenses not covered, or not fully covered by Medicare.

They are sold by private insurance companies.

Medigap Insurance is regulated by both the federal and state governments.

It must be identified as a Medicare insurance supplement.

It must provide specific benefits that help fill the gaps in your Medicare coverage.

* * *

WHEN TO BUY

The best time to buy a Medigap policy is during your Medigap **"open enrollment"** period.

This takes place for a period of 6 months **from the date you are first enrolled in Medicare Part B, and are 65 or older.** You then have the right to buy the policy of your choice.

During this "open enrollment" period,

You cannot be turned down

You cannot be charged higher premiums because of poor health

Once the "open enrollment" period ends, you may not have a choice, and may have to accept whatever Medigap policy an insurance company is willing to sell you.

Now, what if you have Medicare Part B, but are **under 65**? Then the "open enrollment" period begins when you hit 65. Some States will allow the enrollment period earlier.

Check with your state insurance counseling office. They can also advise you of other types of supplemental insurance such as Medicare SELECT, sold by insurance companies and HMO's throughout most of the country.

* * *

A-B-C-D-E-F-G-H-I-J

No, this is not the start of the famous alphabet nursery rhyme. Rather, they are the ten letter-designated insurance plans developed by the National Association of Insurance Commissioners, and incorporated into federal and state law.

Plan "A" is the "basic" Benefit package

All Medigap-certified insurers **must make Plan "A" available.** They do not have to offer the other nine plans, although most will make some, if not all plans, available.

States may regulate the number of plans the insurance companies can offer over and above **Plan "A"**.

Further, residents of Massachusetts, Minnesota and Wisconsin have alternative standardized programs which were in effect prior to the legislation enacted by Congress.

Chart of the Ten Standard Medicare Supplement Plans

Medicare supplement insurance can be sold in only 10 standard plans. This chart shows the benefits included in each plan. Every company must make available **Plan A**. Some plans may not be available in your state.

Basic Benefits: Included in All Plans.
Hospitalization: Part A coinsurance plus coverage for 365 additional days after Medicare benefits end.
Medical Expenses: Part B coinsurance (generally 20% of Medicare-approved expenses).
Blood: First 3 pints of blood each year.

A	B	C	D	E	F	G	H	I	J
Basic Benefit	Basic Benefit	Basic Benefit	Basic Benefit	Basic Benefit	Basic Benefit	Basic Benefit	Basic Benefit	Basic Benefit	Basic Benefit
	Part A Deductible	Part A Deductible	Part A Deductible	Part A Deductible	Part A Deductible	Part A Deductible	Part A Deductible	Part A Deductible	Part A Deductible
		Part B Deductible			Part B Deductible				Part B Deductible
		Skilled Nursing Coinsurance	Skilled Nursing Coinsurance	Skilled Nursing Coinsurance	Skilled Nursing Coinsurance	Skilled Nursing Coinsurance	Skilled Nursing Coinsurance	Skilled Nursing Coinsurance	Skilled Nursing Coinsurance
		Foreign Travel Emergency	Foreign Travel Emergency	Foreign Travel Emergency	Foreign Travel Emergency	Foreign Travel Emergency	Foreign Travel Emergency	Foreign Travel Emergency	Foreign Travel Emergency
			At Home Recovery			At Home Recovery		At Home Recovery	At Home Recovery
				Part B Excess (100%)	Part B Excess (80%)		Part B Excess (100%)	Part B Excess (100%)
							Basic Drug Benefit ($1,250 Limit)	Basic Drug Benefit ($1,250 Limit)	Extended Drug Benefit ($3,000 Limit)
				Preventive Care					Preventive Care

19

SHOPPING FOR MEDIGAP INSURANCE

Things to keep in mind when shopping for Medigap Insurance.

The insurance company must use a standard uniform chart, and outline of coverage, to summarize benefits

They must use the same format, language and definitions

These requirements make it easier for you to compare policies. It also means that each company's plan offerings are alike. So what distinguishes one company from another? What you look for in any company - Service - Reliability - Price!

First thing to do then, is to check out the reliability of the insurer. Then compare premiums and benefits.

* * *

PREMIUMS

While the benefits are identical for plans of the same type, premiums can vary greatly. There are 3 different methods used to figure premiums:

Issue Age Method

You pay the same premium they charge people who are 65, regardless of your age

Attained Age Method

Premium is based on your current age and increases as you get older

No Age Rating

Everyone pays the same premium regardless of age

Rates are regulated by the State. The insurance company can raise your premiums only when it has approval to raise the premiums for everyone else with the same policy.

* * *

BENEFITS

Medigap policies generally pay the same supplemental benefits regardless of your choice of health provider. If Medicare pays for a service, wherever it may be provided, then the standard Medigap policy must pay its regular share of benefits.

* * *

REMARKS

Your State Insurance Counseling Office is the place to go for information on insurance companies licensed to sell you health insurance, suspected violations or fraud, and other insurance complaints.

Also request a free copy of the -

"Guide to Health Insurance for People with Medicare"

See the appendix for a listing of State Insurance Counseling Offices, and their telephone numbers.

CHAPTER 4

- MEDICAID -

HEALTH CARE'S LAST RESORT BUT YOU SHOULDN'T KNOW FROM IT

"It's no shame to be poor, but it's no honor either"

But it is a shame if you can't afford to pay for health care or the insurance premiums to cover you in case of illness.

If you are like me, you probably were brought up to believe that any time you needed help from the government, you were asking for welfare. You would rather die before doing so.. But times have changed. Seniors are living longer. Many of us run out of the financial assets we expected would last us through old age, or the rest of their lives. So what to do? Die of shame, or die from the lack of medical help? Neither! Apply for Medicaid!

HOW MEDICAID DIFFERS FROM MEDICARE

Medicare is a federal health plan run through Social Security.

Medicaid is a joint federal and state medical assistance program that helps needy people pay for medical care. It also pays for medical services needed to protect their health.

It is administered by the state, under the guidelines set by the federal Health Care Financing Administration.

WHO QUALIFIES

A person may have both Medicare and Medicaid, with Medicaid helping to pay for expenses not covered by Medicare.

Eligibility and coverage may differ from State to State. Persons who may receive Medicaid include those -

> Age 65 or older....blind or disabled....families with dependent children....relatives of deprived children.

Medically and financially needy regardless of age, including pregnant women.

INCOME OR ASSETS LIMITS

Family income and/or assets cannot exceed the limits set by the State.

Those include cash, bank accounts, property, social security, pensions etc., You must **first** use these resources, including medical or hospital insurance.

What can or cannot be taken away from you

Federal regulations permit States to attach your estate to recover Medicaid funds expended towards your care. However, not all do. Check what your particular State does in regards to Estate Recovery. In general, at least while you are alive, they won't touch -

- Your Home
- One Car
- Personal Belongings
- Funeral Funds (if made irrevocable)

COVERAGE

In addtion to the standard hospital and medical coverage provided under Medicare, Medicaid recipients would get additional benefits -

- Nursing Home Care
- Prescription Drugs
- Eye Glasses
- (Limited) Dental Care
- Home Health Services
- Other Doctor, Outpatient Services

So it seems that having less (financially), gets you more (benefits). But, not without its cost - emotionally and otherwise.

* * *

HOW TO APPLY

Contact your local or State Department of Social Services (or similar name), and request an application form.

You can authorize someone to act for you.

You or your representative may be called down for an interview, and asked to bring down papers, records and other proof of need.

Medicaid rules are complicated. Get information or help from people with Medicaid knowledge such as The **Area Agency on Aging, and the Social Security Office.** Booklets on Medicaid are available from Social Security.

Free legal help may also be available. Check with local social services organizations or your State Bar Association.

* * *

Just remember, it is no shame you find yourself in financial straits. It is a shame if you need health care for you or your dependents, and are not getting it. Help is available, now that you know where to find it.

CHAPTER 5

MANAGED CARE PLANS OR HMO'S

The cost of healthcare has skyrocketed. No question the government is concerned. No question these factors have given rise to HMO'S. No question that government has been encouraging beneficiaries to move into a managed healthcare plan, since their emphasis is on cutting costs. But, today, even they are having a problem containing costs.

What Is It?

Simply put, an HMO is a combination insurance company and doctor/hospital. There are different types of plans and combinations, but essentially, this is what an HMO is.

It contracts with Medicare to provide all of Medicare's benefits. However, there are differences which you must understand.

* * *

Choice: Fee-For-Service versus Managed Care

Medicare is a *"fee-for-service"* system.

You have your choice of most any doctor, hospital, or healthcare provider.

A fee is usually charged for each service used.

Medicare pays its share of the bill.

You are responsible for the balance, either personally, or through your Medigap supplemental insurance.

* * *

Managed Care works differently. It does manage your care.

- Choice is not yours to make

- You must use their plan's doctors, and health providers, except in emergencies

- They, not your doctor, can make important medical decisions affecting your health and course of treatment

- They can limit access to specialists

* * *

Regardless of which choice you make, you still retain all of your Medicare protections, benefits and appeal rights.

How Managed Care Works

You pick a Plan in your area. In return, the Plan covers all of Medicare 's benefits, plus others. HMO's emphasize preventive care.. There is little or no paperwork involved.

You pay the Plan a fixed monthly premium, and generally a co-payment every time a service is provided. These costs vary from Plan to Plan, and may change each year.

You do **not** pay any of Medicare's deductibles or co-insurance.

But, you must continue to **pay** Medicare's **Part "B"** premium, which is deducted, automatically, from your Social Security check.

A Managed Care Plan can save you money. Do investigate the various Plans in your area, carefully. Then decide if it is for you or if it is not.

Pro's and Con's

Here are some things to consider when checking out plans:

Is your doctor or specialist in the Plan?

Is your hospital of choice in the Plan?

If they are not, will you be happy with a strange physician or hospital belonging to the Plan, especially if you have a chronic condition?

On the plus side, consider these advantages:

- Cost Savings! Medigap insurance isn't needed.

- No extra charges (over and above the co-pay charge) no matter how many times you visit a doctor or use other covered services

- Extra benefits such as - prescription coverage eyeglasses - hearing tests - routine physicals

Other Considerations

Other factors to consider when checking out Plans:

- Area of Plan's Coverage
- Emergency Coverage Within and Outside the Plan's Area
- Foreign/Overseas Coverage

This is important if you travel a lot, take vacations outside the country, or live in another State part of the year.

Remember this!

Medicare does **not** pay for overseas emergency coverage, nor in Canada, nor in Mexico, except under certain conditions.

* * *

TYPES OF MANAGED CARE PLANS

The usual managed care plan has either a **"Risk"** or a **"Cost"** contract with Medicare. There is an important difference.

RISK PLANS

This means you receive all covered care and referrals through the Plan. If you go for service on your own outside the Plan's providers, without authorization, neither the Plan nor Medicare will pay. In short, you are locked in to their rules.

The exceptions to the above are for emergencies inside or outside the Plan's area of coverage.

Another exception offered by some Risk Plans is called the-

POS option or **"Point-0f-Service"**

This option allows certain services outside the plan's providers. However, in exchange, you have to pay at least 20% of the bill.

* * *

COST PLANS

Permits you to go either to the Plan's providers or others outside the Plan. While the Plan will probably not pay for the outside services, Medicare will. However, you will be responsible for Medicare's co-insurance deductibles and other charges just as in their fee-for-service system.

So, under a Cost Plan, you do have some flexibilty.

* * *

Note
Under review by the government, are Plan Choices, patients' rights, and moving in or out of an HMO. Check for changes. See Directory in Appendix.

* * *

HOW TO ENROLL in AN HMO

- You must have **Medicare Part "B"**

- You must continue to pay Part "B" premiums

- You must live in the Plan's area of coverage

- You cannot be receiving Hospice Care at time of enrollment

- You cannot have permanent kidney failure at time of enrollment

All Plans under contract with Medicare must have an advertised **"open enrollment"** period of 30 days, at least once a year.

Plans must enroll Medicare beneficiaries in the order of application.

Medicare beneficiaries cannot be rejected because of poor health.

Coverage must be provided for the first 90 days when traveling.

* * *

What Happens If You Move Out of the Plan"s Area?

Then you will have to leave that Plan. But, you have 2 options.

1. You can return to Medicare
   - or -
2. Enroll in a new Plan serving your new address.

* * *

HOW TO LEAVE AN HMO

You can stay in an HMO as long as it has a Medicare contract. Or, you can leave any time to join another Plan.

If you have decided to return to Medicare:

Send a written request to the Plan, your local Social Security office, or, if appropriate, to the Railroad Retirement Board.

Your return is effective, the first day of the following month - after the Plan receives your request to disenroll. If you are enrolling in another Medicare-contracted Plan, the procedure is simple. You are automatically dis-enrolled from the old one when you sign up for the new one.

* * *

WHAT TO DO ABOUT YOUR MEDIGAP INSURANCE

If you are planning to leave Medicare for an HMO, you won't need your supplemental insurance. **BUT -**

don't be in a rush to discard it.

Suppose, after a short time, you find you are not happy and want return to Medicare. Well, chances are you won't be able to get the same Medigap policy you had originally, especially if you had one of the better ones, and especially if you have a health problem.

The experts advise holding on to your Medigap policy for a trial period, or until you have determined to stick with the HMO.

* * *

Sources of Information

State Insurance Counseling and Assistance Programs can provide general information about Managed Care Plans.

See the directory in the appendix covering **Medicare Carriers, Insurance Counseling, (PRO's) Peer Review Organizations, and Durable Equipment Regional Carriers.**

Lastly, you can contact the **Health Care Financing Administration Regional Offices** for assistance. Their regional offices are also listed in the appendix.

CHAPTER 6

LONG TERM CARE, NURSING HOMES, INSURANCE, and YOU SHOULDN'T KNOW FROM IT

This is a chapter, you'd just as soon skip, because the prospects are not what anyone wants to contemplate. Nevertheless, it behooves you to learn what is involved, where to go for information and help, and what resources are available to you.

* * *

LONG TERM CARE

First, a few points to remember:

1. Medicare does **not** pay for **"custodial"** care (daily assistance needed for dressing ,eating, hygiene, etc)

2. Medicare coverage for **(SNF) Skilled Nursing Facility care** is limited. You, as well as the facility, must meet their qualifications. There are costs you have to pay.

    An alternative to a Nursing Facility, if you meet Medicare's requirements, is **Home Health Care,** which is covered by **Part "A"** of your Medicare Insurance. If you do not have **Part "A"** coverage, then **Part "B"** takes over.

3. Medicaid can help pay for long term care, but first you must meet the poverty level standard established by the government, or have exhausted your resources, which amounts to the same thing.

The majority of nursing home residents are on Medicaid....Their average age - mid-eighties...average "stay" is 2-1/2 to 5 years.

Government legislation in the near future will result in changes in Medicare and Medicaid. Whether they will be for the better, and whether they will address the serious need for a Long Term Care program remains to be seen.

NURSING HOMES

WHEN A HOME IS NOT A HOME

One of the greatest fears we face, as Seniors, is the fear of having to spend our final years in a nursing home. And, as we are living longer, that fear increases, the older we get.

To what extent does the Nursing Home Industry contribute to those fears? Well, consider that, today, nursing homes are big business, run by mostly for-profit companies..... where there are not enough facilities, and where sufficient staff and trained aides are in short supply. That gives rise to problems and abuses.

In 1995, *"Consumer Reports"* magazine, published a series of articles based upon a national, year-long investigation of nursing homes. Here are two of their conclusions:

1. *"The quality of care at thousands of the nation's nursing homes - **is poor or questionable at best..**"*

2. *"About **40%** of all facilities certified by HFCA (Healthcare Finance Administration) have **repeatedly violated Federal standards** over the last four inspection surveys, including standards on critical aspects of patient care....."*

Quite an indictment! Have things gotten better since then? Evidently, not much. Violations, complaints, and abuses abound.

For example:

An April "98 **"60 Minutes" TV** piece highlighted a large, California Nursing home chain that evicted 250 Medicaid residents. Evidently they weren't as profitable as private-pay patients who could otherwise use the vacated beds. The ensuing hue and cry, and bad publicity, caused them to relent, and they offered to take back some of the residents.

Recently, my local television news broadcast the horror story of a temporary aide who became so angry at a resident, he beat him brutally, breaking bones in his face and causing him to be hospitalized.

Other stories tell of residents wandering off from Homes. Some occurred in the winter. In at least one case, the resident died of exposure.

The problems have been on-going, for a number of reasons, not all of them the fault of Nursing Homes.

Legislators have been looking at reforms, at stricter enforcement of government standards regarding health, nutrition, the inside environment, and staffing.

Advocacy groups are on the rise, and so is the number of volunteer groups whose mission is to improve conditions for Nursing Home residents.. Things should improve in the future, but the problems are never going to be eliminated entirely.

* * *

When Considering A nursing Home -

    A. **Tour the entire Home**
    B. **Try to visit at Mealtimes**
    C. **Observe relations between residents and staff**
    D. **Check services and amenities provided**
    E. **Ask about the Staff**
    F. **Check for Government Accreditation**
    G. **Is the Home's License and *Inspection Report posted in a conspicuous place?**

*Your best information may be the State's Inspection Reports. If the Home cannot provide you with the latest report, or past history, contact your State Ombudsman for Nursing Home Residents (usually a department or agency under the State's Department on Aging, or Human Resources). See listing in Appendix.

NURSING HOME CHECKLIST

Choosing a Nursing home requires careful thought and investigation.

The following checklist will help you in making a choice.

CREDENTIALS
    _ Home have a current State license?
    _ Is the Administrator licensed?
    _ Home certified for Medicare and Medicaid?
    _ State Inspector reports prominently displayed?

THE ENVIRONMENT
    _ Pleasant atmosphere?
    _ Clean? Free of unpleasant odors?
    _ Air conditioning and heating adequate?

THE FACILITY
    _ Do rooms have privacy?

- Adequate closet space?
- Toilet and bathing facilities adequate?
- Provide for the Disabled? For Wheelchairs?
- Do faucets, call buttons, telephones, TV, all work?
- Areas set aside for visitors, for recreation rooms?
- Building easily evacuated in an emergency?

THE STAFF
- Enough Nurses and Aides?
- Available all hours, including weekends?
- Qualified? On-going training, especially of Aides?
- Longevity, and turnover ratio?
- Caring? Respectful attitude towards Residents?
- Resident Physician? Readily available if needed?
- Special care provided for Alzheimer patients?
- Policy on use of physical and chemical restraints?

SECURITY
- Building have Smoke Detectors? Sprinklers?
- Equipped with emergency lighting and power?
- Can confused Residents wander out of building?
- Program for Individual emergencies?
- Program for Building emergecies? Evacuations?

MEALS
- Try one. Well-balanced? Appetizing? Tasty?
- Provide for special dietary needs?
- Accommodate choices, preferences?
- Assist Residents needing help eating?
- Do Residents dine together? Talk or socialize during meals?

ACTIVITIES
- Recreation and Social Activities Program?
- How often? Overseen by qualified Staff person?
- Residents seem involved? Participating?
- Outside activitities, trips offered?
- Programs offered for Residents and Family?
- Community, volunteers, religious groups involved?
- Provision for Religious Services?

SERVICES
- Regular, and emergency medical attention assured?
- Hospital transfer arranged in an emergency?
- Pharmaceutical service available?

- Physical therapy and related services offered?
- Transportation provided?
- Visiting hours reasonable?

COSTS
- How daily or monthly costs compare to other Homes
- Any extra charges? Spelled out?
- Financial and other policies specified in Contract?
- Who controls Resident's Assets?
- What happens if money runs out?

GENERAL
- Water plentiful? Available throughout?
- Residents' Rights Posted?
- Policy regarding Transfers, and Discharges?
- Home in good standing with State Inspectors?
- How would you rate the Home for - Its Environment?
- For the care provided Residents?

* * *

FINANCES & ADMISSION CONTRACTS

If it is planned for the person to have Medicaid and/or Medicare coverage, either on admission, or in the future, you must find out if the Home is **certified** to participate in these programs.

Otherwise, their expenses will not be covered!

If the future source of payment may be Medicaid, find out what is the Home's policy on keeping persons who enter as private-pay residents, and later apply for Medicaid

THE ADMISSION CONTRACT

When you enter a Nursing Home, you will be asked to sign an Admissions Agreement. This is a contract which specifies your legal relationship with the Home. The agreements you make in this contract are very important because they describe - the services you receive - your rights - your responsibilities - and the charges for your care.

Find out if your State requires Nursing Homes to establish a written contract with all residents prior to admission, and again when a previous contract expires, or if the source of payment changes. If not, stipulate that you want this. Further, a copy of the contract should be given to the resident or his/her representative at time of admission.

The Contract must include:

> length of the contract
> services to be provided under the contract and the charges
> any additional charges that may be required and the amo
> who is responsible for the fees
> amount of deposit required
> rights, duties and responsibilities of the Resident

Ask for a copy of their Admission Contract as soon as possible. Most are long and contain legal terms. They may even contain illegal requirements (which a Court would not enforce). Other terms may be legal but not acceptable to you. Therefore, you may want to negotiate changes. So the more time you or your attorney have to review the agreement, the better.

The Contract should indicate the Daily Room Rate and the services it covers. Also a list of optional services and their charges. Find out what services are covered in the Daily Rate. You might be charged extra for common services you assumed would be covered in the daily Rate.

Know the Law

Under federal law, Medicare and Medicaid-approved Nursing Homes cannot require anyone other than the Resident to guarantee payment. Nor can they charge deposits nor pre-admission fees to anyone whose care will be covered by Medicare or Medicaid.

Nursing Home Fact Sheet material courtesy Michigan Citizens for Better Care, rev 04/99

FINDING OUT-OF-TOWN CAREGIVERS

For help in finding caregivers in another city or state, try -

> Your, or your parents' physician
> Local or State social service agencies
> Senior center, church groups and charities
> Local Area Agency on Aging
> Hospital, if parent is being released from one

Publications:

"Care Management: Arranging Long Term Care", **Booklet D1380**

AARP Fulfillment (EE 162)
1909 "K" Street NW
Washington D.C. 20049

* * *

National Council on Aging
600 Maryland Ave. SW, West Wing 100
Washington D.C. 20024

Publishes professional standards for social work case management

* * *

Children of Aging Parents
2761 Trenton Road
Levittown, PA 19056

Publishes national directory of geriatric care-givers & support groups, *"Care Sharing"* - cost $15

* * *

National Ass'n of Private Geriatric Care M'grs.
1315 Talbot Tower
Dayton, Ohio 45402

Membership directory - cost $25

* * *

Other Information Sources:

    Aging Network Services
    4400 East-West H'wy 907
    Bethesda, MD 20814

    (301) 657-4329

                              * * *

    Elder Support Network (Service of the Ass'n of Jewish Family Agencies)

    800- 634-7346

                              * * *

    Family Service America
    11700 W. Lake Drive
    Milwaukee WI 53224

    (414) 359-1040

                              * * *

AARP
For Long Term Care information:

    AARP Health Advocacy Services
    601 "E" Street NW
    Washington DC 20049

                              * * *

For Continuing Care Communties:

    AARP Housing Activities
    (same address as above)

                              * * *

For Nursing Home Information:

> **National Council of Senior Citizens**
> **Nursing Home Information Service**
> **1331 "F" Street NW**
> **Washington DC 20004**

* * *

GENERAL INSURANCE INFORMATION

Policies You Don't Need:

> a. **Specific illness policies** - such as cancer, alzheimer, etc...Medicare covers all illnesses
>
> b. **Additional Medi-gap insurance** - You only need one! Want more coverage? Add to existing policy.

* * *

Insurance Information Sources

> **Your State Department of Insurance**
>
> **Local Area Agency on Aging**

* * *

> **United Seniors Health Cooperative**
> **1331 "H" St. NW, Suite 500**
> **Washington D.C. 20005-4706**
>
> **Useful booklet -*"Long Term Care Insurance:***
> ***To Buy or Not to Buy"* - Cost $2**

* * *

> **National Ass'n of Insurance Commissioners**
> **120 W.12 Street, Suite 1100**
> **Kansas City MO 64105-1925**
>
> **ask for *"Shopper's Guide to Long Term***
> ***Care Insurance"***

* * *

Health Insurance Ass'n of America
1025 Connecticut Ave NW, Suite 1200
Washington D.C. 20036

ask for *"Consumers Guide to*
Long Term Care"

* * *

Note: It is a good idea to check out the reliability of any insurance company. Check your library's reference book - *"Best Ratings"*, **published by A.M. Best & Co.**

* * *

INSURANCE CONSIDERATIONS

If you are looking into Long Term insurance, remember that after age 60, costs are high, and health and coverage restrictions increase. But at whatever age you are considering insurance, check these points with the company:

- Costs

- Do premiums increase with age?

- When coverage starts

- What is the length of coverage?

- Restrictions or limitations

- Home care offered?

- Assisted Living offered?

- What happens if funds run out?

- Would Medicaid be accepted?

When all is said and done, you have to ask yourself, can you afford Long Term Insurance? Would it cover you in the future?

As Seniors increase in number, and live longer, the need for care increases. Nursing Homes will capitalize on that. Consider -

Currently, Nursing Home costs range from a low of $33,000, to an average $50,000, to a high of $73,000 a year. By the year 2030, estimates run to $190,000 annually. Most of us won't be around to worry about it then, but our children may. What will happen? Nobody knows, but it is certainly food for thought.

CHAPTER 7

HOSPICE CARE

IT'S A BUMMER, NO MATTER WHAT

.....but it is also a blessing to both patient and family

What is it

- A program for the terminally ill

- Emphasis is on pain management, not cure

- Services are encouraged to be provided at home, but can be in a special hospice facility

- Provides for counseling, support and respite care

Medicare Coverage

Medicare covers Hospice care under the the following conditions:

- Must be entitled to Part "A"

- Doctor's certification that patient is terminally ill and has 6 months or less to live. This can be extended by doctor's re-certification that patient is terminally ill.

- Care provided in a Medicare-certified Hospice program

- Waive regular Medicare benefits in favor of Hospice care, except for treatment of conditions unrelated to the terminal illness

- All services paid in full, except for limited costs for outpatient drugs, and short-term inpatient care

* * *

Services Covered

- Doctors' services and nursing care

- Medical and social services

- Counseling, to patient and family

- Short term inpatient care:
    a) for pain control and management
    b) for "respite" care* (for family need)

    *on an occasional need basis, and for not more than 5 consecutive days

- Medical appliances and supplies including drugs and biologicals

- Home health aides and homemaker services

- Therapy: physical, speech, occupational

* * *

Eligibility Periods

There are 4 time periods during which a person can elect to opt for hospice care over standard Medicare - two 90 days, one 30 days, and one extended period.

Revoking Hospice Care Coverage

Should a patient decide to revoke his/her hospice care and go back to the standard Medicare benefits, he or she may do so. However, if one decides to revoke hospice care in the 4th period, which is the unlimited extended time period, then one is no longer eligible for hospice care coverage, and must remain in the standard Medicare program.

Medicaid Patients

....are also entitled to hospice care. However, since Medicaid is administered through the State, different requirements must be met. Coverage, though, will be the same. Contact your State Health Agency or your local Area Agency on Aging for details.

HMO Members

....may also elect Hospice care. In this case, Medicare pays for the Hospice services, and pays the HMO for the attending physician services, and for services not related to the terminal illness.

* * *

Hospice Care Programs have risen dramatically, and no wonder. The cost to Medicare for skilled nursing home care versus Hospice care is much less costly. But more important, is the comfort to both patient and family, knowing one's final days will be spent at home where loved ones can give care, or in a setting devoted to pain management and compassionate care.

* * *

Sources of Information

Health Care Financing Administration
7500 Security Boulevard
Baltimore MD 21244-1850

* * *

Area Agency on Aging
(local or regional office)

* * *

National Hospice Organization
1901 N. Moore Street, Suite 901
Arlington VA 22209

(800) 658-8898

* * *

Hospice Education Institute
190 Westbrook Road
Essex CT 06426

(800) 331-1620

* * *

National Institute for Jewish Hospice
8723 Alden Drive, Suite 5107
Los Angeles CA 90048

(800) 446-4448

CHAPTER 8

BLAME IT ON OLD AGE

- YOUR AGING EARS -

Hear ye, hear me -

After age 50, you can expect some loss in hearing ability. By age 60 or 70, as many as 25% of Seniors are hearing impaired.

* * *

TYPES OF HEARING LOSS

Presbycusis (prez-bee-ku'sis)

This is the most common type of hearing loss attributable to aging.

It is due to changes in the delicate workings of the inner ear.

Symptoms are :
- difficulty understanding speech
- possible sensitivity to loud sounds

The decline in hearing ability is gradual, and varies in rate from person to person.

"Don't shout, I'm not deaf", is commonly heard from people with this type of impairment.

* * *

Conduction Deafness

Blockage or impairment of the mechanical movement of the outer or middle ear is the cause of this problem. It results in sound waves not traveling properly through the ear.

Effect? - Voices and other sounds may sound muffled, but your own voice may sound louder than normal, so you may tend to speak softly.

Treatment - if it is due to wax buildup, or extra fluid, flushing the ear should correct the problem. If abnormal bone growth or infection are causes, surgery or medication takes care of the problem in most cases.

* * *

Central Deafness

Damage to the nerve centers within the brain.

Sound levels are not affected, but language comprehension usually is affected.

This type of hearing loss is rare.

Causes may be due to illnesses accompanied with high fever - lengthy exposure to loud noises - drug reaction - head injuries - vascular problems, or tumors.

Central deafness is not treatable. But for some people, special training by an audiologist or speech therapist can be beneficial.

Advances in technology have helped the hearing impaired. Hearing aids for example, have been greatly improved and are designed for the degree of hearing loss.

Even in the worst cases of hearing loss caused by nerve damage past the inner ear, cochlear implants may be an option for hearing improvement.

Factors other than aging that may contribute to hearing loss-

- Sustained exposure to noise and high volume

- Poor circulation due to artheriosclorosis

- Poor diet ..... smoking

Obviously in the latter case, good diet and non-smoking will help stave off hearing problems.

When to See a Doctor or Specialist

Hear are some symptoms that you should check out -

- Persistent Ringing in the Ears - especially pain or a problem in one ear (but occasional ringing is common and nothing to worry about)

- You repeat yourself

- You speak too loudly

If you think you have a hearing problem, or feel the need for an examination, check with your family doctor. He may refer you to an audiologist for hearing tests. Or, he may recommend a specialist. The doctors specializing in the hearing field are known as **Otologists** or **Otolaryngologists**.

* * *

Information Sources

American Academy of Otolaryngologists
1101 Vermont Ave N.W.
Washington D.C. 20005

American Speech-Language-Hearing Ass'n
10801 Rockville Pike, Dept AP
Rockville MD 20852
1-800-638-8255

Office of Scientific & Health Reports
National Institute Of Communicative Disorders
Bldg 31, Room 8AO6
Bethesda, MD 20892

Request Pamphlet, *"Hearing Loss: Hope Through Research"*

- YOUR AGING EYES -

TWO COMMON CONDITIONS

1. **PRESBYOPIA** (prez-bee-oh-pee-ah)

A hardening of the eye lens, making it difficult to focus on close objects.

- Common disorder for the over 50
- Normal change in aging eyes
- Easily corrected with glasses or contact lenses

2. **CATARACTS**

A clouding of the eye's lens. It usually develops gradually. It is common in people over 55. Symptoms include:

- Blurred vision
- Halo around lights
- Sensitivity to sun, bright light
- Poor night vision
- Colors change in appearance

Basic treatment is surgery - removing the clouded lens and replacing with artificial clear one: It is -

- a common operation
- done on outpatient basis
- a short recovery period

Most doctors hold off on surgery until you have difficulty seeing as clearly as you like.

* * *

THREE MORE SERIOUS CONDITIONS

1. **GLAUCOMA**

An increase in the fluid pressure inside the eye that damages the optic nerve, causing side vision to slowly diminish ... can lead to blindness.

- Usually no symptoms until advanced state

- Get regular eye checkups after age 50
- Diabetics should be checked every year
- If there's a family history, get regular checks

2. DIABETIC RETINOPATHY

Damage to the blood vessels that feed the retina.

This is a problem for Diabetics and it requires monitoring by an eye doctor.

3. MACULAR DEGENERATION

A serious condition leading to blindness. The light-sensitive tissue in the central part of the retina deteriorates. Symptoms include:

- Distorted vision ..straight lines look curved
- (See Amsler Grid vision check chart)
- Fuzziness in central vision
- Changes in colors

No corrective treatment at this time. But steps may be taken to slow the process. Magnifying devices may be recommmended to help with reading and other close work.

* * *

REMARKS

- Losing your eyesight is *not* a natural process of aging.
- Regular **checkups** are important

Most vision problems can be corrected or alleviated See an eye doctor immediately, if you experience any problems or changes in vision

Technological advances in equipment and surgery have benefited many people with common or serious conditions. Some day, glasses and contact lenses may become obsolete.

* * *

A WORD ABOUT SUN GLASSES

Did you know your eyes can get sunburned if you are out in the hot sun for long? Yes they can! I'm sure you have experienced pain in the eyes at times, especially if you are around water. The ultraviolet radiation in the sun's rays can give you this sunburn. It's called **photokeratitis**, and though not vision-threatening, leaves the eyes red and sensitive to light. It usually heals up within 24 to 48 hours. But the point is that too much exposure to the sun's ultaviolet rays can be painful, and over the years, can lead to serious eye problems such as cataracts, and possibly macular degeneration.

Protect yourself when out in the sun. Wear a broad hat or cap, together with sunglasses that block out the harmful UV rays.

* * *

Check lenses for protective quality

Since you can't see the sun's rays, how do you know if the many types and colors available to you are safe for your eyes? First of all, federal law mandates that labels on sunglasses reveal how much protection the lenses provide against UV. Second, if you are not sure what the label number means, check with your eye doctor or optometrist. Let them advise you on the best glasses for you, and how to check the lens quality. Don't be misled by price or fashionable appearance. Proper protection is your priority. Lastly, wear your sunglasses even on cloudy days because UV radiation can still be strong.

INFORMATION SOURCES

National Eye Institute
National Institute of Health
2020 Vision Place
Bethseda MD 20892-3655

* * *

American Optometric Association
Communications Center, Dep't Q3
243 North Lindbergh Blv'd
St. Louis MO 63141

Pamphlet: *"Answers to Glaucoma Questions"*

* * *

Association for Macular Diseases
210 East 64th Street

New York, N.Y. 10021

* * *

The Lighthouse, Inc.
111 East 59th Street
New York, N.Y. 10022

* * *

American Foundation for the Blind
11 Penn Plaza, Suite 300
New York, N.Y. 10001

(1-800) - 232-5463

* * *

For information on eye care, eye disorders:

Office of Scientific Reporting
National Eye Institute, Bldg 31, Rm 6A32
Bethesda, MD 20892

* * *

National Society to Prevent Blindness
79 Madison Avenue
New York, NY 10016
Ask for free copy of-
"The Aging Eye: Facts on Eye Care for Older Persons"
(Send self-addressed stamped envelope)

* * *

A free *"Vision Inventory List"* of special products and services for the visually impaired. is available from-
Vision Foundation
2 Mt. Auburn Street
Watertown MA 02172

* * *

American Foundation for the Blind

55

15 West 16th Street - (Check current address)
New York, NY 10011

* * *

Professional societies providing information and literature

American Optometric Association
Communications Division
243 Lindbergh Blvd
St. Louis, MO 63141

* * *

American Academy of Opthalmology
655 BeachStreet
San Francisco, CA 94105-1336

VISION CHECK FOR MACULAR DEGENERATION

Take this self-test with the **Amsler Grid** shown below. The small diagram to the side illustrates the distorted lines sympton.

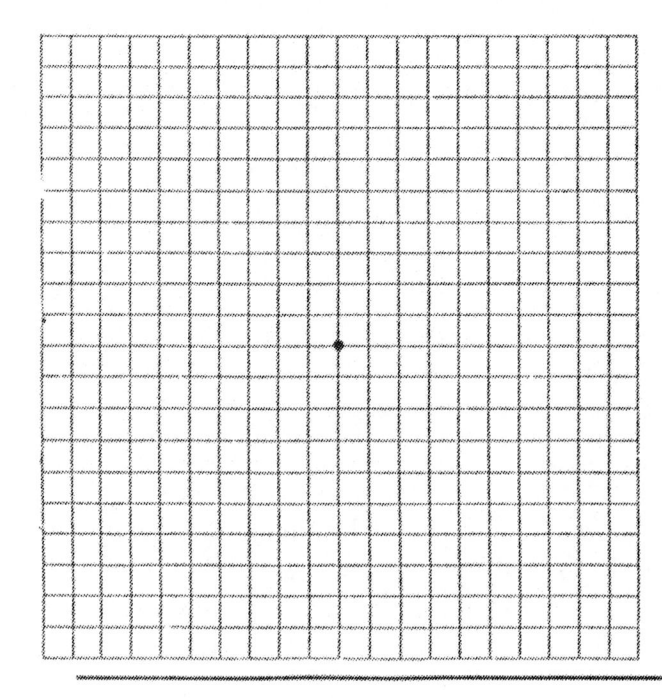

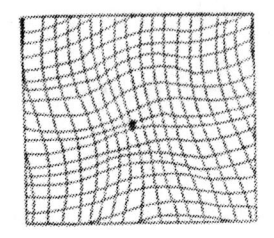

INSTRUCTIONS:
1. Position chart 14" from eye
2. Cover one eye
3. Look directly at dot in center
4. Cover other eye and repeat

AMSLER RECORDING CHART
A replica of Chart No. 1, printed in black on white for convenience of recording.

BENSON OPTICAL COMPANY
1812 Park Avenue, Minneapolis, Minn.

- YOUR AGING SKIN -

Skin Wear, Skin Care

Your skin! It's an organ! The largest of your body! It's with you from day one, until day done.

It takes a lot of abuse. Overexposure to the sun - the ravages of time and weather - the aging process - all take their toll.

Effects of the aging process

As we get older, our skin gets thinner, drier, and wrinkles. Sometimes it almost appears transparent. It loses elasticity. We bruise more easily, take longer to heal. So called (brown) age spots appear - crusty spots and patches. My dermatologist calls these the *"barnacles of aging"* (an apt metaphor).

We can't stem the aging process but we can take steps to slow it down. Proper nutrition, excercise to help tighten the skin, medications and lotions to alleviate dry skin, and periodic checkups with a dermatologist to nip problems in the bud, all are recommended. As a last resort, we can try to fool mother nature with cosmetic surgery. Can't fool her, but the psychological lift it gives people has some health benefit.

* * *

My Sun, My Sun

Most of us are, or have been, sun-worshippers. And the sun, my son, daughter, and the rest of us, is the most damaging to our skin. Even though we learned this later in life, many still continue to bask in the warm sunshine. Bad! Bad! Besides enhancing the afore-mentioned effects of aging, it increases the chances of developing skin cancers.

Skin Cancers on the Rise

The two most common are - **Basal cell carcinoma and Squamous cell carcinoma**

These are the most curable if detected early, and removed in its early stages. Watch for :

* Changes in a mole

* Raw skin, or a sore that doesn't heal

* Any unusual growth

* Color changes in the skin

On the rise, is **Melanoma**, the deadliest of skin cancers. Caught in its early stages, it can be treated.

Here is a simple **A-B-C-D** rule to help you identify and remember important warning signs of skin cancers in general.

    A. **ASYMMETRY** - one half unlike the other.
    B. **BORDER** - irregular...scalloped or poorly defined edges.
    C. **COLOR** - variations...inconsistency...tan, brown, red, black, white, blue.
    D. **DIAMETER** - larger than a pencil eraser.

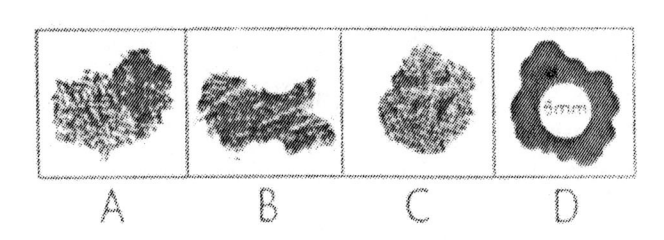

Last but not least, see a Dermatologist once a year for a checkup, and especially if you have ever had a skin cancer.

* * *

SKIN TIPS

* Use a sunscreen with a rating of 15 or higher.

* Avoid prolonged exposure to the sun between 10 a.m. and 3 p.m. when the sun's rays are most intense.

* Wear protective clothing, a hat, UV protection sunglasses.

* Avoid **all** artificial tanning devices and sun lamps.

A word to the wise

The sun feels good, and sun tans look good, but without proper care and precaution, the sun is dangerous to your aging skin.

* * *

PHOTOSENSITIVITY

Did you know that certain medications, or use of topical agents found in some over-the-counter products, can cause a toxic or allergic reaction when you expose yourself to the sun.? It is a condition known as *"photosensitivity"*.

The severity of the reaction is related to the dosage of the drug or amount of the chemicals in a product used. The symptoms in a toxic reaction, for example, can range from changes in skin color, to rashes, blisters, and peeling.

The caution is, if you are going to spend some time in the sunny outdoors, find out from your doctor or pharmacist, if the medications you are taking are photosensitive. Some drugs associated with photosensitivity include certain forms of

...heart medicines.....high blood pressure prescriptions..... antibiotics such as tetracyclines.

Chemicals found in some medicated shampoos, soaps, fragrances and cosmetics, may also trigger a reaction. If you are using any such products, check those out too. For more information on photosensitive medications, contact -

U.S. Food & Drug Administration
Office of Consumer Affairs, HFE 88
5600 Fishers Lane
Rockville MD 20857

Reprint: *"Know the Right Way to Take Your Medicines"*

National Consumers League
815 15th Street N.W., Suite 516
Washington DC 20005

Brochure: *"When Medications Don't Mix"*

* * *

For general skin cancer information:

American Academy of Dermatology
930 N. Meacham Road
P.O. Box 4014
Schaumburg IL 60168-4014

* * *

American Cancer Society

(1-800) ACS-2345

- YOUR AGING TEETH -

You can keep your teeth in your mouth where they belong, for the rest of your life, if you do but three things:

> brush and floss daily

> visit your dentist once or twice a year

> don't wait to see your dentist, if you have any problem

Denture wearers too, must practice good oral hygiene. Changes in the mouth, or loss of bone, can lead to loose fit. Sores can lead to infections as well as cancers of the mouth.

Need for good teeth - real or false

Poor teeth or dentures lead to poor chewing, which leads to poor dietary habits, which leads to poor health. On the other hand, healthy teeth lead to good chewing, and better dietary habits.

Maybe the best thing good teeth can do for you is a healthy smile. This is important to your overall health. A healthy smile makes you look good, makes you feel good, inside as well as outside.

* * *

Things You Should Know

Here is a little quiz for you. True or False? -

1. Plaque is a major cause of tooth decay

2. Plaque is a major cause of gum disease

3. Periodontal gum disease is a major cause of tooth loss

4. Smokers are more prone to gum disease and the consequences are greater than for non-smokers
5. Symptoms of peridontal gum disease include bad taste in mouth, bleeding, loose teeth, teeth spreading apart

The answers to all are - "**true**". If you had even one wrong, especially number 5, run, don't walk, to your nearest dentist.

* * *

Dental Problems

While peridontal gum disease is our most common problem, there are others, such as -

- abrasions...chips...cracks...erosion
- cavities...plaque...staining
- "dry mouth"
- sensitivity to hot and cold
- need for root canal treatment

* * *

Would You Believe

...your dentist can also be something of a detective? For example - are you suffering from stress? A condition known as **"bruxism"** - gnashing or grinding your teeth, which shows up as cracks or worn areas - can indicate to the dentist that stress is the cause.

Oral cancers can be detected, as well as signs of other health conditions such as diabetes.

How about bad breath? Not the kind that comes from eating onions or garlic, or from indigestion, but ba-a-d breath. Bad breath that indicates a serious health condition, such as these odors -

"rotten fish" - possible rare liver disease
"sweet smell" - possible liver disease
"rotten fruit" - denotes diabetes
"nose odors" (due to post nasal drip) - possible nose, ear, or throat problem
possible gum disease

So, next time you go to the dentist, and you think you have a bad breath problem, have a breath checkup too.

* * *

With the tremendous advances in modern dentistry treatment and equipment - sealants, veneers, crowns, caps, implants, cosmetic surgery, and more, - just about any dental problem you have or may have, can be treated or prevented. And, modern dental offices of today are built to accommodate geriatric and wheelchair patients. Today's dentists? - they ain't what they use to be. Check them out, for your good health's sake.

* * *

Information Sources

Information sources on dentistry, other than your local dentist, can be obtained from the -

American Dental Association
211East Chicago Avenue
Chicago, Illinois 60611

Information on dental research is available from-

National Institute of Dental Research
B'ldg. 31, Rm. 2c36
Bethesda MD 20892

CHAPTER 9

- "WHY ME" ILLNESSES -

The three most dreaded words in one's medical vocabulary-

- CANCER -

- HEART DISEASE -

- STROKE -

There are many other debilitating, and fatal illnesses. But these are the most common, and the leading causes of death or impairment. When it strikes, you are very apt to ask, "Why me?".

Luck (bad) plays a part...Genes play a part...Or, maybe both. Are there answers? Some! We still have a long way to go.

The best answer, if you can call it an answer, is the **"preventive"** approach. That entails healthy living - diet and exercise - and regular health checkups. It is no guarantee, but taking better care of ourselves, gives us the ability to better fight these diseases. At the very least, it should provide a better quality of life for the time we have left on this earth. That's a blessing, to be sure.

* * *

- CANCER -

Two kinds do command annual checkups -

**Breast Cancer
and
Prostate Cancer**

Detected early, caught early, these cancers can be treated, arrested, or slowed down significantly.

Medicare now covers both these tests. And, while there may be restrictions on their number and frequency, and whether or not they are considered "checkups" or "diagnostic", should make no difference in your need for them. Make it mandatory to get them.

>**NOTE:** Perhaps we should point out another need for regular cancer checkups - **Colon Cancer** - which has been on the rise in recent years.

* * *

BREAST CANCER

According to the American Cancer Society, every woman is at risk for breast cancer The risk is greater as you get older. Three quarters of all breast cancers occur in women over 50. The risk is also higher if there is a family history of breast cancer.

Detection measures involve   -   annual mammogams
monthly self-exams

Some signs and symptoms to watch for:

>1. A lump or thickening is the most common sign

>Note: most lumps are **not cancerous.** But all lumps should be checked by a doctor. If you feel something, don't wait for your annual checkup. See the doctor, immediately.

>2. Other signs, if they persist -

>>swelling - puckering - skin irritation
pain - tenderness of the nipple

* * *

Resources Providing Support & Greater Understanding

>**American Cancer Society**

>**1-800-ACS-2345**

>**Internet - http://www.cancer.org**

* * *

Y-ME - a support group and information source

1-800-221-2141 (anytime)

Internet - http://www.yme.org

* * *

National Alliance of Breast Cancer Organizations

1-202-296-7477 (anytime)

Internet- http://www.nabco.org

NABCO publishes a newsletter, provides information on patient resources, literature, and support groups

* * *

"Dr. Susan Love's Breast Cancer Book"

**one of the best books on the subject,
very clear...very comprehensive**

* * *

PROSTATE CANCER

The prostate gland is found only in men. Its function is to produce seminal fluid or semen.

As many men die of prostate cancer as do women of breast cancer. Yet thousands walk around unaware of any problem, or the need for regular checkups.

The American Cancer Society, the American Urological Society and other groups feel that a yearly ***PSA** along with a digital **rectal** exam of the prostate should be done for men over fifty.

***PSA** stands for *Prostate specific Antigen"*. It is a blood test designed to **screen** for the presence of prostate cancer. However, it is **not** a cancer test. Only a biopsy, at present, can determine the existence of cancer in the prostate.

PSA is a protein found only in the serum of the prostate. No other part of the body can produce it.

The (finger) Rectal Exam checks the size of the prostate and for suspicious nodules or hardness within the gland. Combined, these tests have dramatically improved doctors' ability to find prostate cancer earlier, and possibly at a more curable stage.

Whether or not earlier diagnosis leads to longer survival is still debatable. Whether or not surgery or cancer treatment is for everyone diagnosed with prostate cancer, depends on one's age and condition. It is something to be discussed with your doctor.

PSA levels

Can be measured. A norm has been arbitrarily set at 4.0. Below this number is generally desired. It applies to most men with normal prostate glands. However, age is a factor which may cause it to be higher.

Other conditions may raise **PSA** levels such as prostatitis (inflammation of the prostate), or -

Benign Prostate Hyperplasia

more commonly known as **BPH.**

BPH is non-cancerous.

It is the most common cause of an elevated PSA level. The majority of older men develop **BPH** to some degree. Simply put, the prostate grows. If it grows too much, you have a problem urinating. If the problem becomes severe, an operation, or use of newer medications may be necessary to reduce the enlargement.

* * *

INFORMATION SOURCES

**Prostate Health Awareness Campaign
P.O. box 2374
Baltimore MD 21203-2374**

(800) 564-6666

* * *

Prostate Health Council
1128 N. Charles Street
Baltimore MD 21201

> Brochure: *"Prostate Cancer: What Men Over40 Should Know"*

* * *

American Foundation for Urologic Disease
300 West Pratt Street
Baltimore MD 21201

> (800) 242-2383

* * *

American Cancer Society Pamphlet,
> *"Facts on Testicular Cancer"*
> (800) ACS-2345

- "WHY ME" -

- CARDIOVASCULAR DISEASE -

Heart disease and Stroke are defined as cardiovascular diseases because both involve the circulatory system.

* * *

HEART DISEASE

....our number one cause of death. Surprisingly, because it usually happens later in life for them, it is also the number one killer of women, and not cancer as we might believe.

Among some common forms of heart disease are:

- Artherosclerosis or hardening of the arteries

- Coronary artery disease - the special arteries that supply blood to the heart itself

- High blood pressure

- Stroke

You are at risk if you:

- have high blood pressure
- have a family history of heart disease

- have diabetes
- smoke, or drink

- are overweight or obese
- don't exercise

- have a high cholesterol level
- don't eat a healthy, balanced diet

Warning signals of a heart attack:

- pressure or pain in the center of the chest lasting 2 minutes or more

- pain spreading to shoulders, neck or arms

- lightheadedness...nausea...shortness of breath may also occur

Sharp, stabbing twinges of pain, that come and go are not usually signs of a heart attack. But don't take chances. Get to a doctor or hospital and get checked.

* * *

Chances of recovery from a heart attack are now greater than ever. But in the event of one, **quick action** is the key. Any of the above symptoms calls for immediate action. Call 911 or your local emergency service, or call an ambulance, or have someone drive you to the nearest hospital emergency room. Choose the fastest of these means to get you there. **Time is of the essence!**

* * *

- STROKE -

What is it?

Simply put, it's a brain attack. It happens when something cuts off the supply of blood to the brain, such as a blood clot. Deprived of oxygen and nutrients, brain cells die.

Like heart attacks, a stroke can happen without warning. In both cases however, conditions have built up over the years that trigger an attack.

Effects

The brain controls body movement. Depending upon where in the brain the stroke occurs, any part of the body can be affected, impairing speech, muscle movement, or other body functions, as well as memory.

* * *

"Ministroke" or TIA - A Warning Sign

A ministroke or TIA (Transient Ischemic Attack) is a temporary attack that can range from seconds, to an average 5 minutes, to up to 24 hours.

While a TIA may not result in permanent neurological damage, it is a warning that a major stroke may be in the offing, or may occur at a later date.

Warning Signals

Like a heart attack, immediate action is necessary.
Know the warning signs:

- Sudden weakness, numbness or paralysis of the face, arm, and leg on one side of the body

- Temporary loss of speech, or slurred speech, or difficulty understanding some one else

- Sudden change in vision, e.g. - dimness...double or blurred vision... flashes of light

- Difficulty swallowing

- Sudden dizziness or balance problem

* * *

As with heart attacks, **time is of the essence.** If you notice any of these symptoms, call your doctor, or get to a hospital, immediately.

Risk Factors

....similar to those for heart attack. Some you can't do anything about, but can be kept in check, like:

- High Blood Pressure
- Diabetes

The following risk factors are very harmful to your vascular system:

- Smoking
- Alcohol and Drug abuse

A change in lifestyle can do wonders, such as:

- Eating right
- Staying Physically Active and Mentally Stimulated

* * *

As we keep saying, detection is the first step to preventing or controlling health problems. That first step is, regular health checkups, or seeing a doctor at the first signs of a problem.

CARDIOVASCULAR INFORMATION SOURCES

American Heart Association
National Center
7272 Greenville Avenue
Dallas TX 75231-4596

1-800 242-1793

Stroke Connection
1-800 242-8271

* * *

National Institute on Aging
NIA Information Center
PO Box 8057
Gaithersburg MD 20898-8057

1-800 222-2225

* * *

National Stroke Association
96 Inverness Drive E, Ste 1
Englewood, CO 80112-5112

1-800-STROKES (787-6537)
Brochure: *"Stroke: Reducing Risk & Recognizing Symptoms"*

* * *

National Heart, Lung, & Blood Institute
P.O. Box 30115
Bethesda, MD 20824-0105

Fact Sheet #55487: *"Stroke Prevention and Treatment"*

* * *

National Institute of Neurological
Disorders & Strokes
P.O. Box 5801
Bethesda, MD 20824
1-800-352-9424

* * *

HYPERTENSION OR HIGH BLOOD PRESSURE

.... Affects approximately 50 million Americans

.... About one third don't even know they have it

Which is why it is often called the "Silent Killer"

What is blood pressure?

Your heart is like a pump. When it beats, it pumps blood into your arteries and creates pressure in them. This pressure causes the blood to flow to all parts of the body.

We all have blood pressure. We need it to live. It varies throughout the day depending upon our activity and other factors.

What is High Blood Pressure?

Normal blood pressure falls within a range. It is not a set number.
An average for normal adults is -

less than 140/90

If your pressure is **consistently** higher than the average, you have High Blood Pressure.

What causes it? Nobody knows!

We're talking about **primary or essential** high blood pressure, the most common form. (secondary high blood pressure caused by illness or some condition, will disappear once the illness is cured.)

Is there a cure?   No!

Can it be controlled?   Yes!

There are excellent drugs available. But work closely with your doctor, particularly in relation to your medications in order to avoid adverse drug interactions.

Take them as prescribed

Advise the doctor if you experience adverse reactions to the medication. It may have to be changed or the dosage modified

Never stop taking your medication without advising your doctor

Have your pressure checked periodically

Controlling your blood pressure will lower your risk of getting a heart attack, stroke, kidney disease. It is a lifelong endeavor, but certainly worth doing. Beats the alternative!

Other controllable and remedial factors

Some other things you can control, preferably under the guidance of your doctor:

Obesity

Eating too much salt (sodium)

Amount of alcohol consumed

Lack of exercise

Stress

Incidentally, stress (aka "tension") is not a synonym for Hypertension, the medical term for high blood pressure.

* * *

INFORMATION SOURCES

**National High Blood Pressure
Information Center
120/80 Nat'l Institutes of Health
Bethseda MD 20014**

**National High Blood Pressure
Education Program
P.O. Box 30105
Bethesda MD 20824**

* * *

American Heart Ass'n
7320 Greenville Avenue
Dallas TX 75231

* * *

DIABETES

Another example of a disease many people are walking around without knowing it. Or, if there are warning signs, too often they are dismissed or ignored as a temporary passing condition.

Unfortunately, if not attended to, diabetes can lead to heart attacks, foot and leg amputation, kidney damage, blindness , even death. Checkups and early treatment are essential.

What is it?

When glucose (sugar) builds up in your blood instead of going into the body's cells.

> When you eat, your body turns the food into glucose.
> Glucose is what fuels the body's cells.

> Insulin helps the glucose get into the cells.

Is it curable? - No!

Controllable? - Yes!

* * *

Risk Factors you can't control:

> **Heredity** - a family history of diabetes

> **Race** - the risk is greater for Blacks, Hispanics, American Indians, and Arab-Americans

> **Age** - although it can strike at any age, including children the risk increases over age 45

Risk Factors you can control:

> **Overweight**

> **Lack of exercise**

> **Poor nutrition**

Warning signs:

>   **Extreme thirst**
>
>   **Blurred vision**
>
>   **Frequent urination**
>
>   **Unusual tiredness or drowsiness**
>
>   **Unexplained weight loss**

* * *

Controlling Diabetes Requires Constant Vigilance!

>   **Point** - You will **always have** Diabetes! Accept that!
>
>   **Point** - With good treatment, your glucose levels may go down to normal again.
>
>   >   **Does it mean you are cured ? No!.**
>   >   **Does it mean you can relax? No!**

The three major factors in controlling your diabetes are :

>   **Good diet plan**
>
>   **Exercise**
>
>   **Weight loss**

The doctor and dietitian or nutritionist can work out a good treatment plan. If that isn't enough, then the doctor may also have to prescribe medication , or insulin shots.

Whatever the plan, **follow it to the letter - daily!** It is easy to fall off the wagon, so to speak, especially if you are feeling good. For example, getting careless with your food and gaining a few pounds can immediately cause problems.

So constant vigilance is the price you pay for good health. But, in the case of diabetes, it is a price worth paying.

* * *

INFORMATION SOURCES

American Diabetes Association
1660 Duke Street
AlexAndria VA 22314

1-800 DIABETES (342-2383)

Internet: WWW.DIABETES.ORG

* * *

American Dietetic Association
National Center for Nutrition & Dietetics
216 West Jackson Boulevard
Chicago, IL 60606-6995

1-800 366-1665

* * *

Re: Diabetic Retinopathy:

National Eye Institute
2020 Vision Place
Bethesda MD 20892-3655

Pamphlet: *"Diabetic Retinopthy"*

* * *

ALZHEIMER'S DISEASE

Arguably, the most feared of all diseases of older Americans because most victims are over 65. Not only is it one of the leading causes of death, the impact - emotionally and financially - upon the afflicted and their families is so devastating that it has been referred to as the *"disease of the century"*.

What is it?

.....a progressive, degenerative, fatal brain disease that interferes with memory, mental abilities, loss of control over body functions.

It is   - **not senility nor a symptom of old age**

   not easily diagnosed

   not currently curable

* * *

Symptoms

Early symptoms vary and may be slight. Over time, they become more noticeable and more intense. They include:

   memory problems - forgetting names, places, things, chores, getting lost

   difficulty doing familiar tasks

   difficulty expressing one's thoughts

   mood or personality changes

* * *

But is it Alzheimer's?

One of the reasons Alzheimer's is hard to diagnose is that similar symptoms may be caused by related forms of dementia, by drug interactions, by kidney problems, depression, and numerous other conditions. Many of those are curable, or treatable.

Extensive medical tests can discover the other causes of what appear to be Alzheimer-like symptoms. But as for Alzheimer's, itself, there are no current tests that can diagnose it with certainty during the patiient's lifetime.

Hopefully, research will come up with an answer or treatment for this dreaded disease. In the meantime, families and caregivers need education, relief, respite and support to enable them to carry on with the burdens imposed upon them.

※ ※ ※

INFORMATION & RESEARCH -

National Institute on Aging/AD
Bldg 31, Room 5C35
Bethesda MD 20205

1-800- 438-4380

* * *

Office of Scientific & Health Reports
Bldg 31 Room 8A16
National Institutes of Health
Bethesda MD 20205

* * *

Alzheimer's Association
919 N. Michigan Avenue
Suite 1000
Chicago IL 60611-1676

1-800- 272-3900

* * *

Support)   **ADRDA**
Group)   70 East Lake Street
              Chicago IL 60601

              1-800- 621-0379

CHAPTER 10

- HOUSING -

A house is not a home if you are alone, or could use help around the house, or help with medications and personal hygiene. Or if you are concerned about your future, how you would manage if your health deteriorates.

There are a number of housing resources available to Seniors and the Elderly. These include:

- Assisted Living
- Continuum of Care
- Continuing Care Retirement Centers

- Independent Housing
- Nursing Homes
- Respite Care/Vacation

- Shared Housing
- Subsidized Housingavailable.

They may provide or make available supportive services.

Who provides these types of housing?

- Government Agencies
- Non-Profit Organizations
- Private Developers

* * *

A. ASSISTED LIVING

1. Adult Foster Care Homes (AFC)

Provide room and board, 24 hour daily supervision, in a small group residential setting.

AFC Homes are generally licensed and regulated by the State. Some homes may accept government aid funds. Others are private pay only.

2. Homes For The Aged (HFA)

Provide room and board, 24 hour supervision, to persons age 60 and older who need assistance, but not nursing home care.

Licensed by the State. Some homes accept government aid funds. Others are private pay only.

3. Private Developments

May offer meals, housekeeping, medication and personal care assistance, social activities and transportation.

Cost of services may be included in rent or available at extra cost. Not required to be licensed.

B. **CONTINUING CARE RETIREMENT COMMUNITIES (CCRC)**

Several levels of housing and care - from independent living to assisted living to nursing home care. Sometimes called *"Lifetime Care"* communities, if they guarantee housing and services for life, once admitted.

Require admission qualifications, substantial entry fees, plus monthly services fees.

Note: for information on CCRC's - who. what. where, and rating - contact:

Continuing Care Accreditation Commission

1-202 - 783-2860

C. **CONTINUUM OF CARE RESIDENCES (CCR)**

Differ from **CCRC's** in that they **do not** guarantee care for life, or the availability of higher levels of intensive care. Generally, do not require substantial entry fees.

D. **INDEPENDENT HOUSING**

Follow same guidelines for any private rental housing, except that they are restricted to Senior tenants. May upcharge for services, amenities, and activities.

E. **NURSING HOMES - 2 TYPES**

   1. **Basic or Custodial**

      For people who **do not** require 24-hour care, but need help with meals and personal care.

   2. **Skilled Nursing Care**

      For people needing 24-hour supervision, and intensive medical care and treatment by licensed nurses or therapists.

      Admission must be referred to by a doctor

      Nursing homes are generally licensed and overseen by the State.

   Nursing homes are expensive, ranging from $25,000 - 45,000 and up, per year. Medicare does not cover custodial care, and provides only limited coverage for skilled nursing homes. They can eat up your finances in a short time. It's a major problem with no current relief in sight. Various insurance plans are offered but they are expensive, and coverage may not outlast your need.

   Medicaid may cover nursing home admission, but strict guidelines must be met. The majority of nursing home residents, at present, are on Medicaid.

F. **RESPITE CARE/VACATION**

   For the relief of care-givers, short term residential facilities are offered by some Nursing Homes, Homes for the Aged, and Adult Foster Homes.

   Requirements vary. Fees usually paid for by private funds and include room and board, 24-hour supervision, personal care assistance and activities.

   A day's respite program is offered by some hospitals and senior centers for a reasonable fee.

G. **SHARED HOUSING**

   1. **Private**

      Help find roommates for a fee.
      Work with people of all ages.

2. Government-Sponsored

No fees .... Match people with similar needs, interests, background and personality.

Requirements - independent Senior, 60 or older.

Check with local Area Agency on Aging, or Social Services Agency for information or assistance.

H. SUBSIDIZED HOUSING

Provide rental assistance to low and moderate income persons. Rents are generally 30% of tenant's adjusted monthly income. Applicants are generally capable of independent living.

Apply to:

Local participating developments

Local HUD (Housing & Urban Development)

State Housing Development Authority

Preference given to disaster or abuse victims, the homeless, or persons paying 50% or more of their monthly income for rent.

* * *

RECOMMENDED BOOKS:

"The 50 best retirement places in America"
- Fred & Alice Lee

* * *

"The 50 healthiest places to live and retire in the United states"
- Norman D. Ford

CHAPTER 11

PENSION PLANS - WHERE'S THE MONEY?

Are you, or have you been a pension plan member of a -

- Government
- Railroad
- Large Corporation
- Small Business

> Are you having difficulty accessing those funds?
> Are you entitled to those funds as a widow, divorcee, or dependent of the pensioner?
> Where do you go for help or assistance?

* * *

PROTECTION UNDER THE LAW

Three agencies to know when checking out a pension plan:

1. **U.S. Department of Labor**

    ... is charged with enforcing **ERISA** - an acronym for the **Employee Retirement Income Security Act.**

    It sets minimum standards for pension plans set up by private industry, and defines the employee's rights, safeguards and guarantees under the law.

    ERISA does not protect all plans. Public plans such as government and Keogh plans, and certain others may not be protected.

2. **Internal Revenue Service**

    ....responsible for seeing that pension plan funding and vesting requirements are met, and for compliance with federal tax laws.

3. **Pension Benefit Guaranty Corporation**

   .....a non-profit, government-funded agency that insures private sector *defined-benefit pension plans.*

* * *

TYPES OF PLANS

We should define the two basic kinds of pension plans since not all are protected under the law:

1. **Defined-Benefit Plans**

   ...promise a specific benefit amount at retirement

2. **Defined-Contribution Plans**

   ...do **not** promise a specific amount. That depends upon amounts contributed and returns on investment. Contributions may come from the employer, the employee, or a combination of both.

* * *

COMMON PROBLEMS & QUESTIONS

1. **How do I find a missing pension?**

2. **Do I have any protection or rights under -**

   - Bankruptcy
   - Merger
   - Plan Changes
   - Disability Before Retired
   - Left company but had "Vested" interest (reached earned pension income stage)

3. Do I have any rights as a -

- Spouse
- Widow(er) Survivor Benefits
- Divorcee
- Remarried Spouse
- Dependent

* * *

SOURCES OF HELP

The Pension Benefit Guaranty Corporation

The **PBGC** is the agency that provides an insurance safety net, against **private defined-benefit** plans that may stop paying, or close down, and answers questions about your benefits. Contact -

> **Coverage & Inquiries Branch**
> **Pension Benefit Guaranty Corp.**
> **2020 "K" Street NW**
> **Washington DC 20006-1806**
>
> **(202) 778-8800**

* * *

For information about terminated plan guarantees -

Pension Benefit Guaranty Corporation
Administrative Review & Technical Assistance
1200 "K" Street N.W.
Washington DC 20005

(202) 326-4000

* * *

OTHER SOURCES OF HELP

For copies of company and union plan summaries and financial statements, contact -

Public Disclosure Room N-5507
Pension & Welfare Benefits Admin.
U.S. Department of Labor
200 Constitution Ave, N.W.
Washington DC 20210

(202) 523-8771

* * *

If you have difficulty getting information from a Company, or need answers to general questions about pension rights, contact -

Division of Technical Assistance & Inquiries
Room N-5625
Pension & Welfare Benefits Admin.
U.S. Department of Labor
200 Constitution Avenue, N.W.
Washington DC 20210

(202) 219-8776

* * *

If you think your pension money is being mismanaged, contact a Labor Department field office, or the -

Pension & Welfare Admin.
Room 558
1730 "K" Street N.W.
Washington DC 20006

(202) 254-7013

* * *

LEGAL SERVICE PROGRAMS

Pension plan rules and claims are very complicated. A lawyer may be needed to sort it out for you.

For Free Legal Assistance

Under the **"Older Americans Act",** if you are at **least 60 years** old, you may qualify for free legal assistance. Look in the phone book under a listing such as *"Legal Assistance to the Elderly",* or *"Legal Services for Seniors".*

* * *

A legal aid program of **AARP,** the American Association of Retired People operates a *"Legal Hotline for Older Americans".*
The hotlines provide legal information, advice, service and referrals to **all** Seniors.......Low income callers will be directed to free legal service programs available.....Others may be directed to cooperating attorneys who charge reduced fees. Contact -

> **AARP**
> **Legal Counsel for the Elderly**
> **601 "E" Street NW**
> **Bldg "A", 4th floor**
> **Washington DC 20049**
>
> **(202) 434-2120**

* * *

Lastly, check with your local **Area Agency on Aging** which can point you to state and local programs available.

Finally, a few words of advice -

> **Record- keeping** is very important. Save and keep track of plan papers, no matter how old.

> Inquiries should be **in writing** and sent **"certified mail"**.

With over 900,000 plans started since **ERISA** was enacted in 1974, it is no wonder that the average time to resolve cases ranges from 2-4 years. The word is, "Patience". Don't give up!

CHAPTER 12

- FITNESS FIGHTS AGING -

"Use it or lose it" - Hippocrates*

Yes, Hippocrates, father of modern medicine, said it way back then, about 2400 years ago (although not that concisely). If you don't stay physically active, your body will run down. Incidentally, Hippocrates practiced what he preached. He lived to the ripe old age of 83 which, for his day, was practically as old as Methusaleh.

Medical Thinking Has Changed

Time was when sufferers of arthritis, asthma, high blood pressure, stroke and heart attacks, were told to limit their activity and get used to a sedentary lifestyle. Now, exercise is routinely prescribed for these people. Today, the medical profession believes:

- Exercise is necessary for maintaining good health
- All things being equal, exercise can slow down the aging process

- Exercise can improve your mental well-being
- You're never too old to start

Consider -

- The man in his fifties who took up walking, then running, then doing marathons into his nineties.
- The woman who took up dancing at age 70, still swinging and swaying at age 95.
- The number of Seniors doing exercise walking, runs into the millions, and increases every year.
- The number of both men and women competing in the Senior Olympics, keeps increasing each year. Amazing, too, are the records both sexes are setting in track, field, and team sports.

Many elderly people think they are too old or frail to exercise. Not so! A university study of nursing home residents showed that these residents improved physically after only a few weeks of moderate exercise and muscle strengthening.

The fact is, that loss of strength and stamina, heretofore attributed to aging, is in part, caused by reduced activity.

* * *

What Kinds of Exercises Recommended

That depends upon your age and physical condition. The best all-around exercise program will include some forms of -

- Aerobics
- Stretching
- Muscle Strengthening

Exercise does not have to be vigorous, nor sustained for a long period of time, nor cause pain. You work within your limits.

For the homebound, the elderly, the frail, or disabled, there are moderate forms of exercise, including chair exercises, that can be performed. These can be done in ten minutes or less, overall, and include exercises for the fingers, hands, arms, and legs. In fact, just lifting one's self halfway out of a chair and down again for a few times, is a great exercise for the arms and legs. There is hardly any one who can't do some exercise, no matter how little, and derive some benefit. It's that important.

Here's a great, **free** book on exercise, motivation and safety -

"Exercise: a Guide from the National Institute on Aging"

It includes many exercises with illustrations and directions. See the "Sources of Information" section on how to get this booklet #NIH 99-4258, plus other valuable material.

Finally, there are any number of exercise videos on the market specifically for Seniors. They range from vigorous to moderate exercises, as well as high to low impact aeorobics.

* * *

Check yourself out, first

We are not going to try to outline an exercise regimen for you. That would be wrong. (The *Activity Pyramid* included in this chapter is for reference only.)

Before undertaking **any** exercise program, the first thing you should do is check with your healthcare practitioner . Next, go to a fitness gym, hospital or wellness center, the local "Y", or other. Check with their fitness experts. If they have an exercise physiologist or trainer, so much the better. Let them work up a program for you that is in keeping with your age and your physical condition. Lastly, **make exercising a habit,** like brushing your teeth.

Take walking, for example. It's one of the best exercises. It's easy! It's natural! You have been doing it all your life. You don't need lessons. Just keep on moving every day !

* * *

You know when it's time to start an exercise regimen?

- *"When your back goes out more than you do"*

- *"When most everything hurts, and that which doesn't - doesn't work!"*

- *"When you sit in your rocking chair and can't get it started!"*

* * *

For any one interested in Hippocrates's actual quote, here it is:

"Speaking generally, all parts of the body which have a function, if used in moderation, and exercised in labors to which each is accustomed, become thereby - healthy and well-developed, and age slowly.....but if unused and left idle, they become liable to disease, defective in growth, and age quickly"

— Hippocrates (460? - 377 B.C.)

- INFORMATION SOURCES -

Publication No. NIH 98-42587
National Institutes of Health
Bldg 31, room 5C27
31 Center Drive, MSC 2292
Bethesda MD 20892-2292

Information Center: **(800) 222-2225**

Internet: **http://www.nih.gov/nia**

* * *

If you have **arthritis, osteoporosis, other musculoskeletal** conditions, or had a hip replacement, free publications on safe exercises for these conditions are available from -

    American Academy of Orthopedic Surgeons
    P.O. Box 1998
    Des Plaines IL 60017

    (800) 824-BONES

                                     *   *   *

    Arthritis Foundation
    P.O. Box 7669
    Atlanta GA 30357-0669

    (800) 283-7800

                                     *   *   *

For **Diabetics** -
    American Diabetes Association
    1660 Duke Street
    Alexandria VA 22314

    (703) 549-1500

free pamphlets: *"Exercise and Diabetes"....."Starting to Exercise"....."20 Steps to Safe Exercise"*

For the **Heart** -
    American Heart Association
    National Center
    7272 Greenville Avenue
    Dallas TX 75231-4596

    (800) AHA-USA1

                                     *   *   *

American Physical Therapy Association
111 North Fairfax Street
Alexandria VA 22314-1488

(800) 992-2782

request -*"For the Young at Heart"*

* * *

For the **Disabled** -

Disabled Sports USA
451 Hungerford Drive
Rockville MD 20850

(301) 217-0960

* * *

Exercises Especially for **Women** -

U.S. Public Health Service
Office on Women's Health
200 Independence Avenue SW, Room 728F
Washington DC 20201

(800) 994-9662

* * *

A REPORT OF THE SURGEON GENERAL

PHYSICAL ACTIVITY AND HEALTH

THE LINK BETWEEN PHYSICAL ACTIVITY AND MORBIDITY AND MORTALITY

* * *

Regular physical activity, performed on most days of the week, improves health in the following ways:

=======	Reduces the risk of dying prematurely
How	Reduces the risk of dying prematurely from heart disease
Activity	Reduces the risk of developing diabetes
Impacts	
Health	Reduces the risk of developing high blood pressure
======	Helps reduce high blood pressure in people who already have it
	Reduces the risk of developing colon cancer
	Reduces the feeLings of depression and anxiety
	Helps control weight
	Helps build and maintain healthy bones, muscles, and joints
	Helps older adults become stronger, and better able to move about without falling
	Promotes psychological well-being

* * *

Millions of Americans suffer from illnesses that can be prevented or improved through regular physical activity.

=======	13.5 million people have coronary heart disease
Health	1.5 million people suffer a heart attack in a given year
Burdens	8 million people have adult-onset diabetes
That	(non-insulin dependent diabetes)
Can Be	
Reduced	95, 000 people are newly diagnosed with colon cancer
Through	each year
Physical	250, 000 people suffer from hip fractures each year
Activity	50 million people have high blood pressure

========   Over 60 million people are overweight

source: U.S. Department of Health and Human Services
        Centers for Disease Control and Prevention
        National Center for Chronic Disease Prevention and Health Promotion
        The President's Council on Physical Fitness and Sports

Examples of Moderate Amounts of Activity

NOTE: Less Vigorous, More Time ========	Washing and waxing car for 45 - 60 minutes Washing windows or floors for 45 - 60 minutes Playing touch football for 30 - 40 minutes Playing volleyball for 45 minutes Gardening for 30 - 45 minutes Wheeling self in wheelchair for 30 - 40 minutes Walking 1-3/4 miles in 35 minutes (20 min/mile) Shooting basketball baskets for 30 minutes Cycling 5 miles in 30 minutes Fast social dancing for 30 minutes Pushing a stroller 1-1/2 miles in 30 minutes Raking leaves for 30 minutes Walking 2 miles in 30 minutes (15 min/mile) Water Aerobics for 30 minutes Swimming laps for 20 minutes Wheelchair basketball for 20 minutes
======== More Vigorous, Less Time ========	Playing a basketball game for 15-20 minutes Bicycling 4 miles in 15 minutes Jumping rope for 15 minutes Running 1-1/2 miles in 15 minutes (10 min/mile) Shoveling snow for 15 minutes Stairwalking for 15 minutes

ACTIVITY PYRAMID FOR SENIORS

Do things you enjoy * Age is NOT a factor * Check with a Doctor first * Let an exercise expert design a program just for you

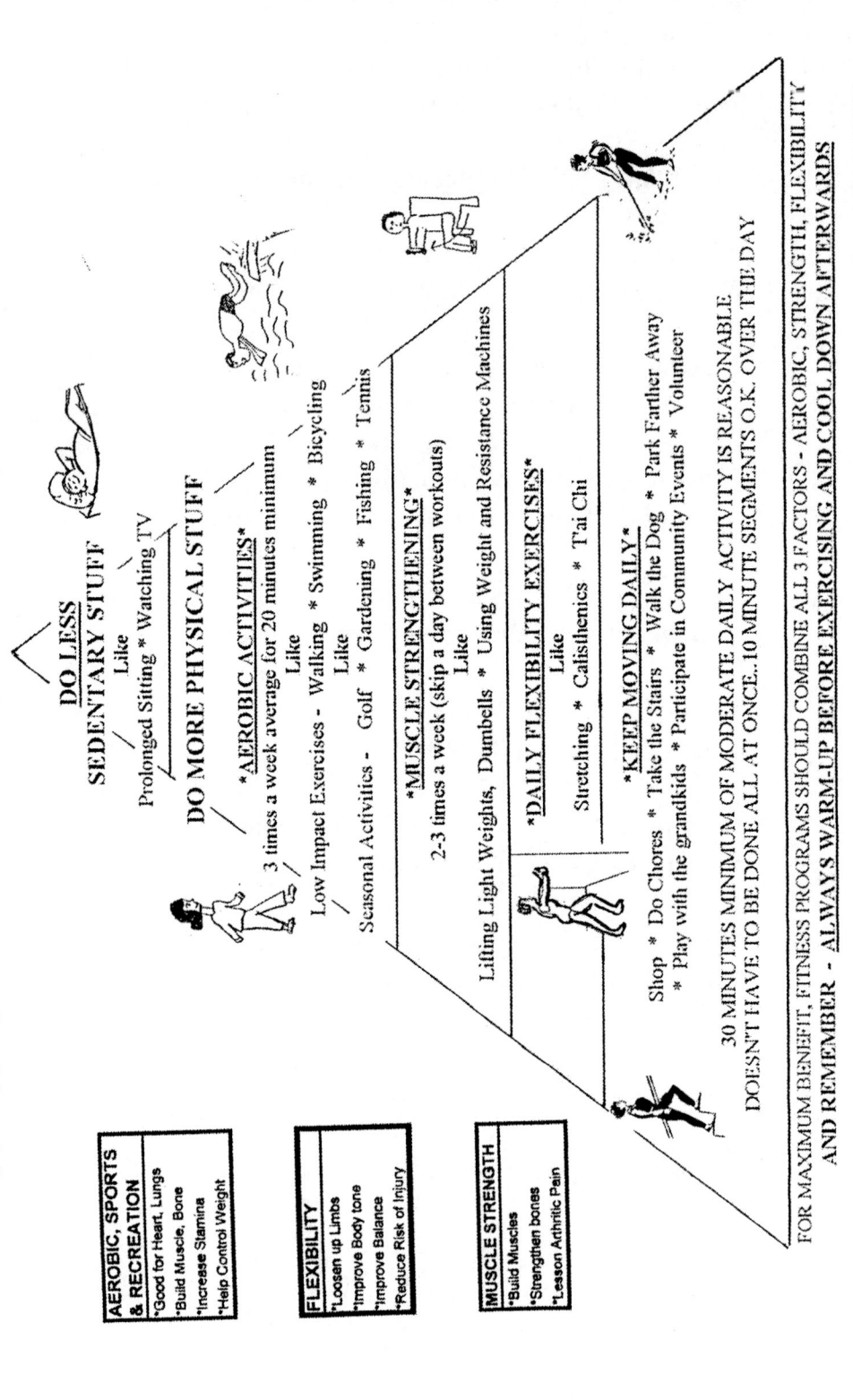

DO LESS
SEDENTARY STUFF
Like
Prolonged Sitting * Watching TV

DO MORE PHYSICAL STUFF

AEROBIC ACTIVITIES
3 times a week average for 20 minutes minimum
Like
Low Impact Exercises - Walking * Swimming * Bicycling
Like
Seasonal Activities - Golf * Gardening * Fishing * Tennis

MUSCLE STRENGTHENING
2-3 times a week (skip a day between workouts)
Like
Lifting Light Weights, Dumbbells * Using Weight and Resistance Machines

DAILY FLEXIBILITY EXERCISES
Like
Stretching * Calisthenics * Tai Chi

KEEP MOVING DAILY
Shop * Do Chores * Take the Stairs * Walk the Dog * Park Farther Away
* Play with the grandkids * Participate in Community Events * Volunteer

30 MINUTES MINIMUM OF MODERATE DAILY ACTIVITY IS REASONABLE
DOESN'T HAVE TO BE DONE ALL AT ONCE..10 MINUTE SEGMENTS O.K. OVER THE DAY

© SOS PUBLICATIONS

AEROBIC, SPORTS & RECREATION
*Good for Heart, Lungs
*Build Muscle, Bone
*Increase Stamina
*Help Control Weight

FLEXIBILITY
*Loosen up Limbs
*Improve Body tone
*Improve Balance
*Reduce Risk of Injury

MUSCLE STRENGTH
*Build Muscles
*Strengthen bones
*Lesson Arthritic Pain

FOR MAXIMUM BENEFIT, FITNESS PROGRAMS SHOULD COMBINE ALL 3 FACTORS - AEROBIC, STRENGTH, FLEXIBILITY
AND REMEMBER - ALWAYS WARM-UP BEFORE EXERCISING AND COOL DOWN AFTERWARDS

FITNESS PLUS GOOD NUTRITION FIGHT FATNESS

Exercise and good nutrition go hand in hand for better health, and a better quality of life. If you have an illness or medical condition requiring special dietary needs, then, of course, that should be worked out with your doctor or nutritionist.

Instead of talking about cholesterol, weight, calories, diets, etc., let's just concentrate upon *"good"* and *"bad"* foods.

Again, a chart is included for your guidance. It requires no explanation. It is recommended by the American Heart Association and the medical establishment. Follow it, together with an exercise program, and, barring any unforeseen situations, you should live longer, and feel better.

Let me end this with a chuckle from a centenarian - Eubie Blake, famous pianist and ragtime composer, who violated all the usual rules of good health practices -

> *"If I had known I was going to live this long, I'd have taken better care of myself"*

* * *

Food Guide Pyramid

A Guide to Daily Food Choices

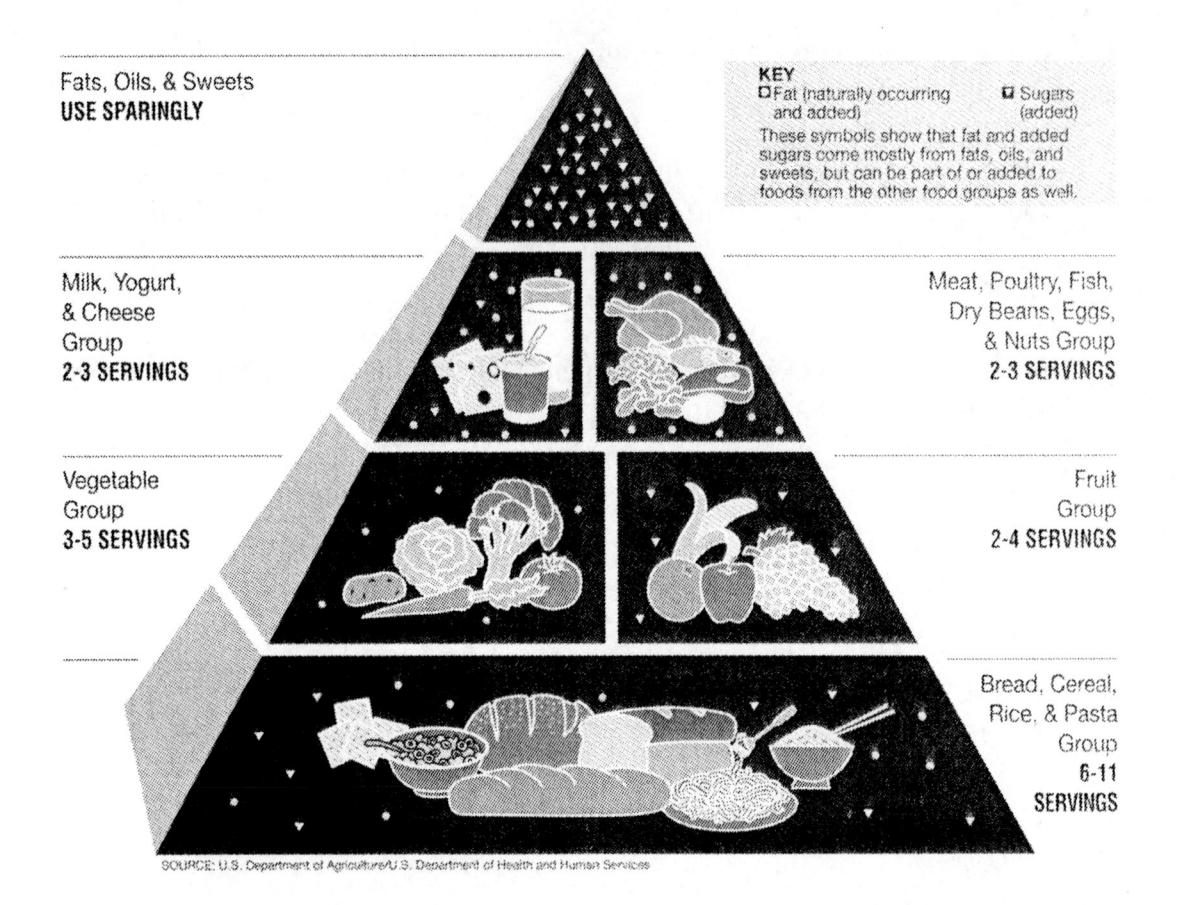

Fats, Oils, & Sweets
USE SPARINGLY

KEY
- ☐ Fat (naturally occurring and added)
- ▪ Sugars (added)

These symbols show that fat and added sugars come mostly from fats, oils, and sweets, but can be part of or added to foods from the other food groups as well.

Milk, Yogurt, & Cheese Group
2-3 SERVINGS

Meat, Poultry, Fish, Dry Beans, Eggs, & Nuts Group
2-3 SERVINGS

Vegetable Group
3-5 SERVINGS

Fruit Group
2-4 SERVINGS

Bread, Cereal, Rice, & Pasta Group
6-11 SERVINGS

SOURCE: U.S. Department of Agriculture/U.S. Department of Health and Human Services

Use the Food Guide Pyramid to help you eat better every day...the Dietary Guidelines way. Start with plenty of Breads, Cereals, Rice, and Pasta; Vegetables; and Fruits. Add two to three servings from the Milk group and two to three servings from the Meat group.

Each of these food groups provides some, but not all, of the nutrients you need. No one food group is more important than another — for good health you need them all. Go easy on fats, oils, and sweets, the foods in the small tip of the Pyramid.

To order a copy of "The Food Guide Pyramid" booklet, send a $1.00 check or money order made out to the Superintendent of Documents to: Consumer Information Center, Department 159-Y, Pueblo, Colorado 81009.

U.S. Department of Agriculture, Human Nutrition Information Service, August 1992, Leaflet No. 572

How to Use The Daily Food Guide

What counts as one serving?

Breads, Cereals, Rice, and Pasta
1 slice of bread
1/2 cup of cooked rice or pasta
1/2 cup of cooked cereal
1 ounce of ready-to-eat cereal

Vegetables
1/2 cup of chopped raw or cooked vegetables
1 cup of leafy raw vegetables

Fruits
1 piece of fruit or melon wedge
3/4 cup of juice
1/2 cup of canned fruit
1/4 cup of dried fruit

Milk, Yogurt, and Cheese
1 cup of milk or yogurt
1-1/2 to 2 ounces of cheese

Meat, Poultry, Fish, Dry Beans, Eggs, and Nuts
2-1/2 to 3 ounces of cooked lean meat, poultry, or fish
Count 1/2 cup of cooked beans, or 1 egg, or 2 tablespoons of peanut butter as 1 ounce of lean meat (about 1/3 serving)

Fats, Oils, and Sweets
LIMIT CALORIES FROM THESE especially if you need to lose weight

> The amount you eat may be more than one serving. For example, a dinner portion of spaghetti would count as two or three servings of pasta.

How many servings do you need each day?

	Women & some older adults	Children, teen girls, active women, most men	Teen boys & active men
Calorie level*	about 1,600	about 2,200	about 2,800
Bread group	6	9	11
Vegetable group	3	4	5
Fruit group	2	3	4
Milk group	**2-3	**2-3	**2-3
Meat group	2, for a total of 5 ounces	2, for a total of 6 ounces	3 for a total of 7 ounces

*These are the calorie levels if you choose lowfat, lean foods from the 5 major food groups and use foods from the fats, oils, and sweets group sparingly.

**Women who are pregnant or breastfeeding, teenagers, and young adults to age 24 need 3 servings.

A Closer Look at Fat and Added Sugars

The small tip of the Pyramid shows fats, oils, and sweets. These are foods such as salad dressings, cream, butter, margarine, sugars, soft drinks, candies, and sweet desserts. Alcoholic beverages are also part of this group. These foods provide calories but few vitamins and minerals. Most people should go easy on foods from this group.

Some fat or sugar symbols are shown in the other food groups. That's to remind you that some foods in these groups can also be high in fat and added sugars, such as cheese or ice cream from the milk group, or french fries from the vegetable group. When choosing foods for a healthful diet, consider the fat and added sugars in your choices from all the food groups, not just fats, oils, and sweets from the Pyramid tip.

- INFORMATION SOURCES -

Free booklets about nutrition for older adults, available from -

**United States Dep't of Agriculture
Center for Nutrition Policy
1120 20th street NW
Suite 200, North Lobby
Washington DC 20036**

(202) 418-2312

* * *

**American Diabetes Association
Information Service Center
1660 Duke Street
Alexandria, VA 22314**

(800) 232-3472

* * *

**American Heart Association
7272 Greenville Avenue
Dallas, Texas 75231-4596**

(800) AHA-USA1

CHAPTER 13

HITTING THE ROAD - TRAVEL for SENIORS

"MAY YOU LIVE EVERY DAY OF YOUR LIFE"
                                    - JONATHAN SWIFT

The emphasis is on **l-i-v-e!** One way to do that is to travel.

As a group, Seniors travel more than the rest of the population. They have the time, the money, and the inclination to see the world before they leave it.

Because of this, those in the travel business who recognize the sales potential, offer special deals, and cater to our special needs.

DEALS, DEALS, DEALS

For example, those who are retired can take advantage of Senior discounts, as well as off-season trips, or off-peak travel times, with substantial savings. Where and how to find these bargains? Check the transportation companies directly. Whether your choice is by land, by sea, or in the air, you will be surprised at what you can find, simply by calling and asking about deals. One time, I did just that for a flight from Detroit, to Los Angeles, asking if there were any unsold seats on off-peak or late hour flights. I got one
for about one third the regular cost. Take the first offer unless it sounds too good to be true.. Call back. You will most likely get another agent. He or she may or may not give you a better price . Incidentally, this was with a major airline.

* * *

INFORMATION SOURCES

Getting more popular, every day, are the discount deals offered on the Internet, by both the airlines, and discount organizations which show trips, transportation costs, "specials", everything you could want to know and more. If you do not have a computer with access to the Internet, check with some one who does, or with your local Library. Also check -

- The travel section in your weekend newspaper

- Magazines aimed at Seniors. Many Libraries and Senior Centers stock them (e.g. *"Mature Life"*)

- Travel Agencies. Good ones know about Senior Packages

* * *

THINGS YOU SHOULD KNOW WHEN TRAVELING ABROAD

Medically speaking, find out about:

- Required Immunizations
- Health tips regarding food and water
- Countries or areas dangerous to your health

For detailed information, call the Government's -

**(CDC) Center for Disease Control
(202) 512-1800**

Also available is their reference book -
"Health Information for International Travellers"

 - **Cost $14**

Also good to know -
**The International Association for
Medical Assistance to Travellers**

Offers a free directory of English-speaking doctors in 500 hundred cities around the world.

Also check-

**American Security Card Med-Card Systems
3165 Cahaba Heights Plaza
Birmingham ALA 35243
(800) 962-CARD**

Med-Card contains microfilm of your entire medical history, insurance, and other personal information in case of emergency.

* * *

"World Immunization Chart",
and the
"World Climate Chart"

Both invaluable. Call **(716) 754-4883**

* * *

**International S.O.S Assistance
One Neshaming Interplex
Trevose PA 19047**

(800) 523-8930

memberships by week, month or year
in case of illness, they take charge, arrange to bring patient to the nearest home medical facility

* * *

**Health Insurance - Health Care Abroad
(800) 336-3310**

* * *

More information on traveling abroad is available from -

**Overseas Citizens Services
U.S. Department of State
2201 "C" Street NW, Room 4800
Washington D.C. 20520**

(202) 647 - 5225

* * *

IMPAIRED? DISABLED? YOU CAN STILL ENJOY TRAVELING

The American Disabilities Act really opened up travel in the U.S.A. for the 49 million disabled by ensuring access in all communities, parks and public buildings. Whether you are vision impaired, hearing impaired, or otherwise physically handicapped, there are organizations catering to the disabled, like Accessible Journeys, which plans tours and cruises both here and abroad.

Some foreign countries are not as accommodating to the disabled; some are. You can get information on these from organizations like American Express. Other sources include:

A. **ORGANIZATIONS**

Travelin' Talk Network
Publishes a directory listing agencies specializing in travel for the disabled...van rentals with wheelchair lifts
Cost - $35

* * *

Society for the Advancement of Travel for the Handicapped
(212) 447-7248
Publishes a list of almost 4,000 hotels with special accommodations, as well as a quarterly magazine

* * *

Servas
(212) 267-0252
Lists of 148 countries with homes and hosts able to accommodate disabled travelers

* * *

B. **TOURS**

Accessible Journeys
(800) 846-4537
World-wide tours for mobility impaired

* * *

**The Guided Tour Inc.
(215) 782-1370**
World-wide tours for adults

* * *

**Wilderness Inquiry
(800) 728-0719**
Outdoor adventures for adults and children
with or without disabilities

* * *

C. RENTALS

**Wheelchair Getaways
(800) 642-2042**
Vans with special controls, lifts, custom features

* * *

D. PUBLICATIONS

**Fodor's Travel Guide
"Great American Vacations for
Travelers with Disabilities"
Cost - $19.50**

* * *

**Disabled Travelers Resource Directories
3103 Executive Parkway, Suite 212
Toledo, Ohio 43606**
Trips and travel agents for the disabled

* * *

SPECIAL VACATIONS

There are a number of specialized vacations that combine travel with education; volunteer vacations such as Habitat, adventure trips, whatever your desires and physical condition allows. Here are a few of them:

ELDERHOSTEL
75 Federal Street
Boston, MA 02110-1941
(617) 426-8056

"From Cicero to computers - politics to poetry - from Maine to Manitoba - Wollongong to Wales, Elderhostel offers you the opportunity to take an adventure of the body, mind and spirit".

That's how Elderhostel describes its programs in one catalogue. A non-profit organization, it offers short, inexpensive academic programs in the U.S., Canada, and longer trips abroad. Accommodations vary, from a college dorm, a field research center, or a nearby hotel/motel. As for academic trips, there are no special qualifications (except for a few intensive study programs), no homework or grades. For the hardier Senior, courses combine study of an area, along with field trips.

To enroll in an Elderhostel program, you must be at least 55 years old. A younger spouse or companion can accompany you. My wife and I have enjoyed the trips we've taken immensely. Compared to other types of vacations, these are a bargain. A typical 5-night program in the U.S. averages, currently, about $435, including - Registration, Classes, Room and Board, and extra-curricular activities. Quite a bargain!

Travel expense of getting there is yours (can't have everything). Some people, including your author, plan additional programs or another vacation excursion in the region, before or after the original one. That way, you make the most of an Elderhostel trip.

INTERHOSTEL
University of New Hampshire
6 Garrison Avenue
Durham NH 03824-3529
(800) 225-4570

Developed by the University of New Hampshire, Interhostel offers more than 50 travel/study programs in 25 countries, for the intellectually inclined, and physically active Senior of 50 years up.

Each program has its unique features. Subjects cover a wide range of topics including the history, politics, natural environment and culture of the region, all presented by the faculty and other representatives of the university or educational institution in question. Excursions to sites of historical or cultural significance, planned social activities, enhance the classroom experience.

Courses are usually longer - 2 to 3 weeks. So costs vary depending upon the program and country chosen, but they include airfare and all program expenses.

* * *

VOLUNTEER VACATIONS

What is a volunteer vacation?

"one where you work for some organization or agency on a special project, mostly at your own expense".

Who would do that?

"Lots of people - people who believe in helping others".

If you are one of those, if you want the satisfaction that you have helped others in need, here or in Third World countries, then check out the latest edition of -

"Volunteer Vacations - short term adventures that will benefit you and others"

— Bill McMillon

The book lists over 240 organizations and agencies needing volunteers, the kind of skills required, where needed, costs, etc. Many of the projects are not applicable to Seniors, requiring the health, stamina and physical condition of younger people. But listings and referral sources for Seniors are included.

Project costs vary from under $500 to $2,000 up, depending upon length of stay and location. You could be building houses in Kentucky for Habitat for Humanity; be distributing medical supplies in Guatemala; or teaching English in foreign lands; or working on archaelogical digs, and so on.

* * *

CHAPTER 14

ELDER LAW

As we live longer and grow in numbers, more problems arise with which we must contend such as healthcare claims and appeals, insurance problems, estate planning, retirement, wills, power of attorney, pension benefits, taxes, and many other situations requiring legal assistance or counsel. So it is no wonder that now there are attorneys specializing in **Elder Law.**

* * *

Do You Need an Elder Law Attorney?

That's the first question to ask yourself. Is this a legal problem, or a medical or social services issue that can be resolved by the agency concerned? You can get help in that regard from the Area Agency on Aging, the State and local offices servicing Seniors, or state and local bar associations.

If it is determined to be a legal issue, then find an **Elder Law** attorney, one knowledgeable in your particular situation, since there are many different fields of law. Discuss fees in detail. Legal fees, generally, are expensive. So be sure every aspect is covered. Many lawyers will offer a free initial consultation.

Legal Assistance Programs

If you are 60 years or older, you may qualify for free legal aid programs funded by the **U.S. Administration on Aging**. Check the telephone book under the title of *"Legal Assistance (or Services) to the Elderly"* for the address and phone number of the nearest agency in your area.

If you are a member of the **American Association of Retired Persons,** you can get a free consultation and reduced rates through a network of cooperating attorneys. Contact AARP at-

**AARP Legal Services Network
601 "E" Street, NW
Washington DC 20049**

(800) 424-3410

* * *

The applications of **Elder Law** are too numerous to cover here. Instead, let's look at some basic, but important legal documents that prepare you for emergencies and, for not-liked-to-think-about, but essential end-of-life considerations.

* * *

WILLS

....a legal document that sets forth **how, and to whom**, your possesions and assets are to be distributed after your death.

> Wills **must go through Probate Court** before your estate can be distributed

> Leaving **no Will**, creates legal headaches, not to mention the potential for conflict among surviving relatives.

> **Without a Will, the State takes over** and decides how your assets are to be distributed.

* * *

LIVING TRUST

.....places your assets into a "Living Trust" while you are still alive.

There are these advantages:

> **Avoids** Probate

> Assets go **directly** to heirs

> Can be **revoked** any time you change your mind **Protecting Yourself Before and After**

You can make sure your wishes, your assets, your health and life decisions, are carried out while you are alive as well as after you are gone. You can do this with legal documents. Of course, the best time to create these documents is while you are still healthy and mentally competent. The documents are:

A. **DURABLE POWER OF ATTORNEY**

B. 'LIVING" WILL

* * *

There are 2 types of Power of Attorney. One is for property and financial affairs. The other is for health and medical decisions.

A. DURABLE POWER OF ATTORNEY

1. for Property and Finances

You can specify when durable power goes into effect and protect yourself by having a medical doctor certify when you have become incapacitated and unable to manage your affairs. In this document, you can:

> specify who will be acting for you
>
> who will make decisisons and manage your affairs
>
> who can sign checks, documents, disburse monies

* * *

2. for Health Treatment Wishes

This one enables you to control your medical treatment by specifying your desires in the event you become incapacitated.

> **It insures your treatment choices are honored.**
> In the event of serious, or life-threatening illness, it allows you to

appoint a "proxy" to make life or death decisions.

B. "LIVING" WILL

For End-of-Life Decisions

A **"Living" Will** spells out your wishes regarding medical treatment, or removal of treatment, in the event of a terminal illness, or if on life support, or in a permanent coma.

These wishes could also be included in a Durable Health Care Power of Attorney. A **"Living" Will** covers end-of-life wishes only.

Because of the importance of this document, it should be given very careful thought. It should be discussed in detail with your family and doctors. It should state your desires so clearly that there is no chance for uncertainty or misunderstanding on their part, if the time comes when you are no longer able to speak for yourself. You will also relieve your family of feeling guilty, if they had to make a life-ending decision on their own. It is not the kind of burden you would want to place upon them.

* * *

REMARKS

Re: Changes

It is important to note that the documents discussed **can be changed or modified any time you wish.** It is wise to have changes witnessed and notarized

Re: Updating

Further, they should be reviewed periodically. Why? Because things can and do change as life goes on. There may be a change in marital status. Births, deaths, divorce, a move out of state, a change in assets or property, and other factors, may prompt a need for changes on your part.

It is important to keep these documents current.

- APPENDIX -

PRIMARY SOURCES OF INFORMATION

TOLL-FREE TELEPHONE NUMBERS

THE INTERNET & SENIOR WEBSITES

MEDICARE RESOURCE DIRECTORY

DIRECTORY OF STATE INSURANCE DEPARTMENTS

SOCIAL SECURITY CHANGES IN THE YEAR 2000

MEDICARE CHANGES IN THE YEAR 2000

- APPENDIX -

PRIME SOURCES OF INFORMATION

Consultants get large fees, not for what they know, so much as for knowing where to go for information. But you don't need to hire consultants because we're going to tell you, and most of it is free. First and foremost, check with these two primary sources:

AREA AGENCY ON AGING - There are local, regional and state offices in every State, and in some U.S. Territories . (see listing at end of this chapter)

STATE OFFICE ON AGING (may go by other names in your State such as 'Human Services", etc.)

Your telephone directory should have the addresses and phone numbers of the above, as well as the following **local sources.**

City Or County Human Services Dep'ts

Senior Centers, Religious and Charitable Organizations

* * *

FEDERAL

For answers or referrals about government programs and agencies, contact-

Federal Information Center
P.O. Box 600
Cumberland MD 21502-0600

(800) 688-9889

* * *

U.S. Dep't of Health & Human Services

Various agencies under this department offer information and publications on a wide range of subjects:

National Institute on Aging
Information Center
P.O. Box 8057
Gaithersburg MD 20898-8057

(1-800) 222-2225

* * *

National Health Information Center
P.O. Box 1153
Washington DC 20013-1133

(1-800) 336-4757

* * *

Consumer Information Center
Pueblo, Colorado 81009

A government mail-order operation offering publications on a wide range of helpful consumer information, from benefit programs to health, jobs, child care, travel, you name it. They publish a -

"Consumer Information Catalog"

....from which you can order the publications listed.
call -
(1-888) 878-3256

* * *

OTHER:

AARP - an important advocate and Washington Lobbyist for Seniors..... Offers many programs, publications, information and special services.

AARP
1909 "K" Street N.W.
Washington DC 20049

TOLL-FREE INFORMATION NUMBERS

Just about any question you can think of about Seniors can be answered by some government agency, non-profit organization religious institution, charity, or support group. Which ones, and where to find them is the problem. For starters, here are some toll-free numbers you can check for specific information.

	(800) -
ADMINISTAR (pays Medicare for wheelchairs, walkers, and other approved equipment)	270-2313
AARP LEGISLATIVE INFORMATION	826-8683
ALZHEIMER'S ASSOCIATION	272-3900
ALZHEIMER'S & RELATED DISORDERS	621-0379
AMERICAN CANCER SOCIETY	ACS-2345
AMERICAN CANCER RESEARCH CENTER	525-3777
AMERICAN COUNCIL FOR THE BLIND	424-8666
AMERICAN DIABETES ASSOCIATION	342-2383
AMERICAN FOUNDATION FOR THE BLIND	232-5436
AMERICAN HEART ASSOCIATION	242-1793
AMERICAN KIDNEY FUND	638-8299
AMERICAN ASS'N OF KIDNEY PATIENTS (AAKP)	749-2257
AMERICAN LIVER FOUNDATION	223-0179
AMERICAN LUNG ASSOCIATION	LUNG-USA
AMERICAN PARALYSIS ASSOCIATION	225-0292
AMERICAN PARKINSON'S ASSOCIATION	223-2732
AMYOTROPHIC LATERAL SCLEROSIS (ALS)	782-4747
ASK THE PHARMACIST	258-1245
ARTHRITIS FOUNDATION	283-7800
ASTHMA/ALLERGY F'DN OF AMERICA (AAFA)	727-5400
BLADDER CONTROL	23-SIMON
BETTER HEARING INSTITUTE	EAR-WELL
BETTER VISION INSTITUTE	424-8422
BRAILLE-GRAMS (WESTERN UNION)	325-6000
CANCER INFORMATION CENTER	422-6237
CANCER RESEARCH INSTITUTE	223-7874
CHILDREN OF AGING PARENTS (CAP)	227-7294
CAPTIONED FILMS/VIDEOS FOR THE DEAF	237-6213
CENTER FOR THE PARTIALLY SIGHTED	481-3937
CENTER FOR INDEPENDENT LIVING	482-0222

```
                                                   (800) -
COMELIA DE LANGE SYNDROME FOUNDATION ----------- 223-8355
CROHNS & COLITIS FOUNDATION ------------------------------ 932-2423

DEAFNESS RESEARCH FOUNDATION -------------------------- 535-3323
DRUG ABUSE HOTLINE ------------------------------------------ 662-4357
ELDERCARE LOCATOR SERVICE ----------------------------- 677-1116
ELDER SUPPORT NETWORK ---------------------------------- 634-7346
EPILEPSY FOUNDATION ----------------------------------------- 332-1000
EYE-CARE HELPLINE -------------------------------------------- 222-3937

FOUNDATION FIGHTING BLINDNESS --------------------------- 683-5555
GLAUCOMA RESEARCH FOUNDATION ------------------------ 826-6693
HEALTHCARE SERVICE CORPORATION:
     MEDICARE - PART "A" ------------------------------------ 872-2566
     MEDICARE - PART "B" ------------------------------------ 482-4045

HOSPICE --------------------------------------------------------- 331-1620
HOUSING COMPLAINTS (HUD) ---------------------------------- 424-8590
HOUSING SENIOR HELP LINE ---------------------------------- 327-9148
HUNTINGTON DISEASE HOTLINE ------------------------------ 345-4372
JOB ACCOMMODATION HOTLINE -------------------------------- 526-7234
JOB OPPORTUNITIES FOR THE BLIND ------------------------ 638-7518
LEGAL HOTLINE FOR SENIORS ------------------------------- 347-LAWS
LUNG DISORDERS (ASTHMA, OTHERS) ------------------------ 222-5846

LUPUS FOUNDATION ------------------------------------------- 558-0121
MEDICAID HOTLINE --------------------------------------------- 638-6414
MEDICAID/MEDICARE FRAUD OR ABUSE --------------------- 368-5779
MEDICARE INQUIRY - PART "A" - (HOSPITAL) --------------- 872-2566
     - PART "B" - (NON-HOSPITAL) ----------------------------- 482-4045

MEDICARE APPEALS & COMPLAINTS --------------------------- 365-5899
MULTIPLE SCLEROSIS HOTLINE ------------------------------- 344-4867
NATIONAL CONSUMER FRAUD LINE --------------------------- 876-7060
NATIONAL CYSTIC FIBROSIS FOUNDATION ------------------ 344-4823
NATIONAL FEDERATION OF THE BLIND ----------------------- 638-7518
NATIONAL FRAUD INFORMATION CENTER -------------------- 876-7060
NATIONAL HEAD INJURY FOUNDATION ----------------------- 444-6443
NATIONAL HEARING AID FOUNDATION ----------------------- 521-5247
NATIONAL KIDNEY FOUNDATION -------------------------------- 622-9010
NATIONAL OSTEOPOROSIS FOUNDATION --------------------- 464-6700
NATIONAL SCOLIOSIS FOUNDATION --------------------------- 673-6922
NATIONAL SPINAL CORD INJURY HOTLINE ------------------ 526-3456
```

(800) -

NATIONAL SPINAL CORD INJURY ASSOCIATION ----------- 962-9629

NATIONAL STROKE ASSOCIATION ------------------------------ 787-6537
NURSING HOME LONG TERM CARE ----------------------------- 292-7852
NURSING HOME OMBUDSMAN, OFFICE OF AGING -------- 342-9871
POISON CONTROL -- 764-7661
PRESCRIPTION DRUG CREDIT ---------------------------------- 367-6263

PREVENT BLINDNESS AMERICA --------------------------------- 221-3004
PHYSICALLY IMPAIRED ASSOCIATION ----------------------- 274-7426
RAILROAD RETIREMENT FRAUD & ABUSE HOTLINE ----- 772-4258
- MEDICARE CLAIMS FOR RAILROAD RETIREES ------------ 833-4455

SKIN CANCER FOUNDATION -------------------------------------- SKIN-490
SOCIAL SECURITY ADMINISTRATION ------------------------- 234-5772
　　　　　　　　　　　　　　　　　　　　　　　　　　　　　　　　772-1213
TAXPAYERS ASSISTANCE (FEDERAL) ------------------------- 829-1040
THE LIGHTHOUSE -- 334-5497

THE SIMON FOUNDATION FOR CONTINENCE ------------- 23- SIMON
VETERANS INFORMATION & ASSISTANCE -------------------- 482-0740
VETERANS AFFAIRS -- 827-1996
VISION FOUNDATION -- 852-3029
Y-ME (BREAST CANCER SUPPORT HOTLINE) ---------------- 221-2141

THE INTERNET

There is a whole new world out there for you to explore - an electronic world. It's called *cyberspace"* , otherwise known as the **Internet**. More and more Seniors are discovering it.

Imagine a library with more information for and about Seniors than you knew existed - information that is instantly available when you click on to a particular website, as they are called.

Want to research a medical problem? - Find the best places to retire? - Need information on caregivers? - Looking for a pen pal or a place to chat? - How about a list of inexpensive vacations at home or abroad that cater to Seniors?

This is just a smidgen' of what is available out there.

Most libraries today, have computers. Many give free classes on how to use them and how to access the Internet. Same goes for many schools and colleges. For sure, some one in the family has, or is familiar with the Internet, and can help you.

* * *

Here are a few Senior website addresses and coverage:

Administration on Aging

>Profiles older Americans • Statistical data
>Older Americans Act • The Aging Network
>>http://www.aoa.dhhs.gov/

* * *

AARP (American Ass'n of Retired Persons)

>Links to websites for members & non-members
>>http://www.aarp.org/

Elderhostel

>Elderhostel catalogue with course descriptions, site descriptions, and program availablilty
>>http://www.elderhostel.org/

* * *

Growth House

Information and referral services to agencies working with issues of death and dying
> **http://www.growthhouse.org/**

* * *

RetireNet

Retirement-related interests, including retirement community information
> **http://www.retire.net/**

* * *

Senior Living Alternatives

Nationwide directory of retirement communities, assisted care facilities, and nursing homes
> **http://www.senioralternatives.com/**

* * *

SeniorCom

Includes the Senior News Network, and is listed in the Web's list of *"who's who on the Net"*
> **http://www.senior.com/**

* * *

SeniorNet

Online community of senior computer users over 55
> **http://www.seniornet.org/**

Social Security Administration:

Laws - Legislation - Benefits Information - Offices
http://www.ssa.gov/

* * *

Third Age

Rated one of the best places for Seniors to use the Internet both for information and interactivity
http//www.third age.com/

* * *

Widow Net

Information on issues of grief, daily living, and family topics for those left behind
http://fortnet.org/WidowNet/

* * *

MEDICAL INFORMATION WEBSITES

Health information provided by the U.S. government:
www.healthfinder.gov

* * *

(CDC) Centers for Disease Control
www.cdc.gov

* * *

By the American Medical Association:
www.ama assn.org

These are just a few websites (locations). Just abut every medical association, health association (diabetes, etc), pharmaceutical company, and so on, now can be reached on the Internet.

WHERE TO CALL FOR HELP

Medicare Carriers: Call about Part B bills and services, and fraud and abuse.

Alabama Blue Cross & Blue Shield, 1(800)292-8855	Florida Blue Cross & Blue Shield, 1(800)333-7586 in-state calls only	Louisiana Louisiana Medicare - Part B, 1(800)462-9666 in-state calls only
Alaska Noridian Mutual Insurance Company, 1(800)444-4606	Georgia Cahaba Govt Benefit Adminstr., 1(800)727-0827	Maine National Heritage Insurance Co, 1(800)882-1228
American Samoa Noridian Mutual Insurance Company, 1(800)444-4606	Guam Noridian Mutual Insurance Company, 1(800)444-4606	Maryland Trailblazers, 1(800)444-4606 Also services Fairfax and Alexandria Counties, Arlington, VA
Arizona Noridian Mutual Insurance Company, 1(800)444-4606	Hawaii Noridian Mutual Insurance Company, 1(800)444-4606	Massachusetts National Heritage Insurance Co, 1(800)882-1228
Arkansas Blue Cross & Blue Shield Of Arkansas, 1(800)482-5525 in-state calls only	Idaho Cigna Medicare, 1(800)342-8900 in-state calls only	Michigan Wisconsin Physicians Service, 1(800)482-4045
California Transamerica Occidental Life, 1(800)675-2266 Counties of Los Angeles, Orange, San Diego, Ventura, Imperial, San Luis Obispo, Santa Barbara National Heritage Insurance Co, 1(800)952-8627 Rest of state	Illinois Wisconsin Physicians Service, 1(800)642-6930 Indiana Adminastar Federal, 1(800)622-4792	Minnesota United Health Care, 1(800)352-2762 in-state calls only Mississippi United Health Care, 1(800)682-5417 in-state calls only
Colorado Noridian Mutual Insurance Company, 1(800)332-6681	Iowa Noridian Mutual Insurance Company, 1(800)532-1285	Missouri Blue Cross And Blue Shield Of Arkansas, 1(800)392-3070 St. Louis City and County, Jefferson County, and area 99 Blue Cross & Blue Shield, 1(800)432-0216 out-of-state calls only 1(800)892-5900 in-state calls only
Connecticut United Health Care, 1(800)982-6819 in-state calls only	Kansas Blue Cross & Blue Shield Of Kansas, 1(800)633-1113	
Delaware Trailblazers, 1(800)444-4606 Also services Fairfax and Alexandria Counties, Arlington, VA	Kentucky Adminastar Federal, 1(800)999-7608	Montana Blue Cross & Blue Shield Of Montana, 1(800)332-6146 in-state calls only

Medicare & You 2000

WHERE TO CALL FOR HELP

Medicare Carriers: Call about Part B bills and services, and fraud and abuse.

Nebraska Blue Cross & Blue Shield, 1(800)633-1113	Ohio Nationwide Mutual Insurance Co, 1(800)848-0106	Utah Blue Cross & Blue Shield, 1(800)426-3477
Nevada Noridian Mutual Insurance Company, 1(800)444-4606	Oklahoma Blue Cross And Blue Shield Of Arkansas, 1(800)522-9079	Vermont National Heritage Insurance Co, 1(800)882-1228
New Hampshire National Heritage Insurance Co, 1(800)882-1228	Oregon Noridian Mutual Insurance Company, 1(800)444-4606	Virgin Islands Triple S, 1(800)474-7448 in-state calls only
New Jersey Empire Medicare Services - New Jersey Operations, 1(800)462-9306	Pennsylvania Xact Medicare Services, 1(800)382-1274 in-state calls only	Virginia Trailblazers, 1(800)444-4606 Also services Fairfax and Alexandria Counties, Arlington, VA United Healthcare/Travelers. Ins., 1(800)552-3423 in-state calls only
New Mexico Blue Cross And Blue Shield Of Arkansas, 1(800)423-2925	Puerto Rico Triple S Inc., 1(800)981-7015 in-state calls only	
New York Blue Cross & Blue Shield, 1(800)252-6550 Services upstate NY Empire Medicare Services, 1(800)442-8430 Services downstate NY Group Health Inc., 1(800)632-5572 Queens county only	Rhode Island Blue Cross & Blue Shield Of Rhode Island, 1(800)662-5170 South Carolina Palmetto Government Benefits Administration, 1(800)868-2522	Washington Noridian Mutual Insurance Company, 1(800)444-4606 Washington D.C. Trailblazers, 1(800)444-4606 Also services Fairfax and Alexandria Counties, Arlington, VA
North Carolina Cigna Medicare, 1(800)672-3071 in-state calls only	South Dakota Noridian Mutual Insurance Company, 1(800)437-4762	West Virginia Nationwide Mutual Insurance Co, 1(800)848-0106
North Dakota Noridian Mutual Insurance Company, 1(800)247-2267	Tennessee Cigna Medicare, 1(800)342-8900 in-state calls only	Wisconsin Wisconsin Physicians Service, 1(800)944-0051 in-state calls only
Northern Mariana Islands Noridian Mutual Insurance Company, 1(800)444-4606	Texas Blue Cross & Blue Shield, 1(800)442-2620	Wyoming Noridian Mutual Insurance Company, 1(800)442-2371

Medicare & You 2000

WHERE TO CALL FOR HELP

State Health Insurance Assistance Program: Call about Medicare Supplemental Insurance (Medigap) Policies, Medicare health plan choices, and help with filing an appeal.

Alabama 1(800)243-5463 in-state calls only	Georgia 1(800)669-8387 in-state calls only	Maine 1(800)750-5353	New Hampshire 1(800)852-3388 in-state calls only	Oregon 1(800)722-4134	Vermont 1(800)642-5119 in-state calls only 1(802)748-5182 out-of-state calls only
Alaska 1(800)478-6065 in-state calls only	Guam 1(808)586-7299	Maryland 1(800)243-3425 in-state calls only	New Jersey 1(800)792-8820 in-state calls only	Pennsylvania 1(800)783-7067	
American Samoa 1(808)586-7299 Government of American Samoa	Hawaii 1(808)586-7299	Massachusetts 1(800)882-2003 in-state calls only	New Mexico 1(800)432-2080 in-state calls only	Puerto Rico 1(877)725-4300 in-state calls only	Virgin Islands 1(340)778-6311 X2338
Arizona 1(800)432-4040	Idaho 1(800)247-4422 in-state calls only	Michigan 1(800)803-7174	New York 1(800)333-4114	Rhode Island 1(800)322-2880 in-state calls only	Virginia 1(800)552-3402
Arkansas 1(800)224-6330	Illinois 1(800)548-9034 in-state calls only	Minnesota 1(800)333-2433	North Carolina 1(800)443-9354 in-state calls only	South Carolina 1(800)868-9095 in-state calls only	Washington 1(800)397-4422 in-state calls only
California 1(800)434-0222 or call 800-510-2020 in-state calls only	Indiana 1(800)452-4800	Mississippi 1(800)948-3090	North Dakota 1(800)247-0560 in-state calls only	South Dakota 1(800)822-8804	Washington D.C. 1(202)676-3900
Colorado 1(800)544-9181 in-state calls only	Iowa 1(800)351-4664	Missouri 1(800)390-3330	Northern Mariana Islands 1(808)586-7299 Government of American Samoa	Tennessee 1(800)525-2816	West Virginia 1(877)987-4463
Connecticut 1(800)994-9422 in-state calls only	Kansas 1(800)860-5260 in-state calls only	Montana 1(800)332-2272 in-state calls only		Texas 1(800)252-9240	Wisconsin 1(800)242-1060
Delaware 1(800)336-9500 in-state calls only	Kentucky 1(502)564-7372	Nebraska 1(800)234-7119	Ohio 1(800)686-1578 in-state calls only	Utah 1(800)541-7735 in-state calls only	Wyoming 1(800)856-4398
Florida 1(800)963-5337 in-state calls only	Louisiana 1(800)259-5301 in-state calls only	Nevada 1(800)307-4444	Oklahoma 1(800)763-2828 in-state calls only		

Medicare & You 2000

WHERE TO CALL FOR HELP

Durable Medical Equipment Regional Carrier (DMERC): Call about bills for durable medical equipment and a list of approved suppliers of this equipment.

If you live in:	Your DMERC is:	If you live in:	Your DMERC is:
Illinois Indiana Maryland Michigan Minnesota Ohio Virginia Washington D.C. West Virginia Wisconsin	Administar Federal 1(800)270-2313	Alaska American Samoa Arizona California Guam Hawaii Idaho Iowa Kansas Missouri Montana Nebraska Nevada North Dakota Northern Mariana Islands Oregon South Dakota Utah Washington Wyoming	Cigna Medicare 1(800)899-7095

If you live in:	Your DMERC is:	If you live in:	Your DMERC is:
Alabama Arkansas Colorado Florida Georgia Kentucky Louisiana Mississippi New Mexico North Carolina Oklahoma Puerto Rico South Carolina Tennessee Texas Virgin Islands	Palmetto Government Benefits 1(800)213-5452	Connecticut Delaware Maine Massachusetts New Hampshire New Jersey New York Pennsylvania Rhode Island Vermont	United Health Care - Region A 1(800)842-2052

Medicare & You 2000

WHERE TO CALL FOR HELP

Fiscal Intermediary: Call about Part A bills and services, hospital care, skilled nursing care, and fraud and abuse.

Alabama Mutual Of Omaha, 1(402)351-2860	Georgia Blue Cross & Blue Shield, 1(706)322-4082	Maine Assoc. Hospital Svc. Of Maine, 1(888)896-4997
Alaska Premera Blue Cross, 1(425)670-1010	Guam Hawaii Medical Service, 1(808)948-6247	Maryland Trailblazers, 1(800)444-4606
American Samoa Hawaii Medical Service, 1(808)948-6247	Hawaii Hawaii Medical Service, 1(808)948-6247	Massachusetts Assoc. Hospital Svc. Of Maine, 1(888)896-4997
Arizona Blue Cross Of Arizona, 1(602)864-4298	Idaho Blue Cross Blue Shield/Oregon, 1(503)721-7000	Michigan Wisconsin United Government Services, 1(313)225-8317
Arkansas Blue Cross & Blue Shield, 1(501)378-2173	Illinois Adminastar Federal, 1(312)938-6266	Minnesota Blue Cross & Blue Shield, 1(800)382-2000
California Blue Cross Of California, 1(805)383-2038	Indiana Adminastar Federal, 1(800)622-4792	Mississippi Trispan Health Svcs. /Medicare, 1(800)932-7644
Colorado Blue Cross & Blue Shield, 1(800)442-2620	Iowa Wellmark Blue Cross Blue Shield Of Iowa, 1(712)279-8650	Missouri Trispan Health Svcs. /Medicare, 1(800)932-7644
Connecticut United Health Care, 1(203)639-3222	Kansas Blue Cross & Blue Shield - Part A, 1(800)445-7170	Montana Blue Cross & Blue Shield, 1(800)447-7828X4086
Delaware Empire Medicare Services, 1(800)442-8430	Kentucky Adminastar Federal, 1(800)999-7608	Nebraska Blue Cross & Blue Shield, 1(402)390-1850
Florida Blue Cross & Blue Shield, 1(904)355-8899	Louisiana Trispan Health Svcs. /Medicare, 1(800)932-7644	Nevada Blue Cross Of California, 1(805)383-2038

Medicare & You 2000

WHERE TO CALL FOR HELP

Fiscal Intermediary: Call about Part A bills and services, hospital care, skilled nursing care, and fraud and abuse.

New Hampshire New Hampshire/Vermont Health Service, 1(603)695-7204	**Pennsylvania** Veritus Medicare Services, 1(800)853-1419	**Virginia** Blue Cross & Blue Shield, 1(540)985-3931
New Jersey Horizon Blue Cross & Blue Shield Of New Jersey, 1(973)456-2112	**Puerto Rico** Cooperativa De Seguros De Vida, 1(800)986-5656 in-state calls only	**Washington** Premera Blue Cross, 1(425)670-1010
New Mexico Blue Cross & Blue Shield, 1(800)442-2620	**Rhode Island** Blue Cross & Blue Shield Of Rhode Island, 1(800)662-5170	**Washington D.C.** Mutual Of Omaha, 1(402)351-2860
New York Empire Medicare Services, 1(800)442-8430	**South Carolina** Blue Cross And Blue Shield Of South Carolina, 1(803)788-4660	**West Virginia** Blue Cross & Blue Shield, 1(540)985-3931
North Carolina Blue Cross & Blue Shield, 1(800)685-1512 in-state calls only	**South Dakota** Wellmark, 1(712)279-8650	**Wisconsin** Blue Cross Blue Shield Of WI, 1(414)224-4954
North Dakota Noridian Mutual Insurance Company, 1(800)247-2267	**Tennessee** Blue Cross & Blue Shield, 1(423)755-5955	**Wyoming** Blue Cross & Blue Shield, 1(800)442-2376
Northern Mariana Islands Hawaii Medical Service, 1(808)948-6247	**Texas** Blue Cross & Blue Shield, 1(800)442-2620	
Ohio Adminastar Federal, 1(513)852-4314	**Utah** Blue Cross & Blue Shield, 1(801)333-2410	
Oklahoma Blue Cross And Blue Shield, 1(918)560-3367	**Vermont** New Hampshire/Vermont Health Service, 1(603)695-7204	
Oregon Blue Cross Blue Shield/Oregon, 1(503)721-7000	**Virgin Islands** Cooperativa De Seguros De Vida, 1(800)986-5656 in-state calls only	

Medicare & You 2000

WHERE TO CALL FOR HELP

Regional Home Health Intermediary (RHHI): Call about home health care, hospice care, and fraud and abuse.

If you live in:	Your Regional Home Health Intermediary is:
Connecticut Maine Massachusetts New Hampshire Rhode Island Vermont	Assoc. Hospital Svc Of Maine 1(888)896-4997

If you live in:	Your Regional Home Health Intermediary is:
Alaska American Samoa Arizona California Guam Hawaii Idaho Nevada Northern Mariana Islands Oregon Washington	Blue Cross Of California Medicare 1(805)383-2990

If you live in:	Your number to call about Medicare home health benefits is:
Maryland Washington D.C.	Medicare Customer Service Center 1(800)444-4606

Medicare & You 2000

WHERE TO CALL FOR HELP

Regional Home Health Intermediary (RHHI): Call about home health care, hospice care, and fraud and abuse.

If you live in:		Your Regional Home Health Intermediary is:
Alabama	Georgia	Palmetto Government Benefits
Florida	Mississippi	1(727)773-9225
Arkansas	North Carolina	Palmetto Government Benefits
Illinois	Ohio	1(803)788-4660
Indiana	Oklahoma	
Kentucky	South Carolina	
Louisiana	Tennessee	
New Mexico	Texas	

If you live in:	Your Regional Home Health Intermediary is:
Michigan	United Government Services
Minnesota	1(414)224-4954
New Jersey	
New York	
Puerto Rico	
Virgin Islands	
Wisconsin	

If you live in:		Your Regional Home Health Intermediary is:
Colorado	North Dakota	Wellmark/Blue Cross Blue Shield Of Iowa
Delaware	South Dakota	1(515)246-0126
Iowa	Utah	
Kansas	Virginia	
Missouri	West Virginia	
Montana	Wyoming	
Nebraska		

Medicare & You 2000

WHERE TO CALL FOR HELP

Peer Review Organization (PRO): Call about quality of care complaints and filing an appeal or complaint.

Alabama Quality Assurance Foundation, 1(800)760-4550	Georgia Georgia Medical Care Foundaton, 1(800)979-7217	Maine NE Health Care Quality Foundation, 1(800)772-0151 New Hampshire, Vermont and Maine only
Alaska Pro-west, 1(800)878-7170	Guam Mountain Pacific Quality Health Foundation, 1(800)524-6550	Maryland Delmarva Foundation Medic. Care, 1(800)492-5811
American Samoa Mountain Pacific Quality Health Foundation, 1(800)524-6550	Hawaii Mountain Pacific Quality Health Foundation, 1(800)524-6550	Massachusetts Masspro, 1(800)252-5533 in-state calls only
Arizona Health Services Advisory Group Inc., 1(800)359-9909	Idaho Pro-west, 1(800)445-6941	Michigan Michigan Peer Review Organizan, 1(877)787-2847
Arkansas Foundation For Medical Care, 1(800)272-5528	Illinois Il Found. For Quality Health Care, 1(800)647-8089	Minnesota Stratis Health, 1(877)787-2847
California California Medical Review, 1(800)841-1602	Indiana Health Care Excel, 1(800)288-1499	Mississippi Foundation For Medical Care, 1(800)844-0600
Colorado Foundation For Medical Care, 1(800)727-7086	Iowa Iowa Foundation For Medical Care, 1(800)752-7014	Missouri Patient Care Review Foundation, 1(800)347-1016
Connecticut Qualidigm, 1(800)553-7590	Kansas Foundation For Medical Care, 1(800)432-0407	Montana Mountain Pacific Quality Health Foundation, 1(800)497-8232
Delaware West Virginia Medical Institute, 1(800)422-8804 in-state calls only	Kentucky Health Care Excel, 1(800)288-1499	Nebraska Sunderbruch Corporation, 1(800)247-3004
Florida Fl. Medical Quality Assurance, 1(800)844-0795	Louisiana Louisiana Health Care Review, Inc., 1(800)433-4958 in-state calls only	Nevada Healthinsight, 1(800)748-6773 or 1(800)748-6944

Medicare & You 2000

WHERE TO CALL FOR HELP

Peer Review Organization (PRO): Call about quality of care complaints and filing an appeal or complaint.

New Hampshire NE Health Care Quality Foundation, 1(800)772-0151 New Hampshire, Vermont and Maine only	**Pennsylvania** Kepro, 1(800)322-1914	**Virginia** Virginia Health Quality Ctr, 1(800)545-3814 in-state calls only
New Jersey Peer Review Organization Of NJ, 1(800)624-4557 in-state calls only	**Puerto Rico** Quality Improvement Prof. Rsrch, 1(800)981-5062 in-state calls only	**Washington** Pro-west, 1(800)445-6941
New Mexico Medical Review Association, 1(800)279-6824	**Rhode Island** Rhode Island Quality Partners, 1(800)662-5028 or call 1-800-553-7590 for Connecticut	**Washington D.C.** Delmarva Found. For Med. Care, 1(800)999-3362
New York Ipro, 1(800)331-7767 Appeals	**South Carolina** Carolina Medical Review, 1(800)922-3089 in-state calls only	**West Virginia** West Virginia Med. Instit. Inc, 1(800)422-8804 in-state calls only
North Carolina Medical Review Of North Carolina Inc., 1(800)722-0468	**South Dakota** Foundation For Medical Care, 1(800)658-2285	**Wisconsin** Wisconsin Peer Review Organization, 1(800)362-2320
North Dakota North Dakota Health Care Revew, 1(800)472-2902 in-state calls only	**Tennessee** Foundation For Medical Care, 1(800)489-4633	**Wyoming** Mountain Pacific Quality Health Foundation, 1(800)497-8232
Northern Mariana Islands Mountain Pacific Quality Health Foundation, 1(800)524-6550	**Texas** Texas Medical Foundation, 1(800)725-8315	
Ohio Peer Review Systems, Inc., 1(800)589-7337 in-state calls only 1(800)837-0664 out-of-state calls only	**Utah** Healthinsight, 1(800)274-2290	
Oklahoma Foundation For Medical Quality, 1(800)522-3414 in-state calls only	**Vermont** NE Health Care Quality Foundation, 1(800)772-0151 New Hampshire, Vermont and Maine only	
Oregon Oregon Medical Professional, 1(800)344-4354	**Virgin Islands** V. I. Medical Institute Inc., 1(340)778-6470	

Medicare & You 2000

WHERE TO CALL FOR HELP

State Medical Assistance Office: Call about low-income programs to help pay medical bills.

Alabama 1(800)362-1504	Georgia 1(800)766-4456 in-state calls only	Maine 1(800)321-5557 in-state calls only	Nebraska 1(800)430-3244 Department of Health & Human Services	Ohio 1(800)324-8680	Utah 1(800)662-9651 in-state calls only
Alaska 1(800)211-7470	Guam Number Not Available	Maryland 1(800)685-5861		Oklahoma 1(800)522-0310 in-state calls only	Vermont 1(800)250-8427 in-state calls only
American Samoa 1(808)587-3521	Hawaii 1(808)587-3521	Massachusetts 1(800)841-2900	Nevada 1(800)992-0900 in-state calls only	Oregon 1(800)282-8096 in-state calls only	Virgin Islands 1(877)641-2004 in-state calls only
Arizona 1(800)334-5283	Idaho 1(800)926-2588	Michigan 1(800)292-2550 out- of-state calls only 1(800)642-3195 in-state calls only	New Hampshire 1(800)852-3345 in-state calls only	Pennsylvania 1(800)692-7462 in-state calls only	Virginia 1(804)786-7933
Arkansas 1(800)482-8988	Illinois 1(800)252-8635 in-state calls only		New Jersey 1(800)356-1561	Puerto Rico 1(877)641-2004 in-state calls only	Washington 1(800)562-3022
California 1(800)952-5253	Indiana 1(800)433-0746 in-state calls only	Minnesota 1(800)366-5411	New Mexico 1(800)432-6217 in-state calls only	Rhode Island 1(401)222-7000	Washington D.C. 1(202)727-0735
Colorado 1(800)221-3943	Iowa 1(800)972-2017	Mississippi 1(800)421-2408 in-state calls only	New York 1(518)486-4803	South Carolina 1(803)898-2500	West Virginia 1(304)926-1700
Connecticut 1(800)842-1508 in-state calls only	Kansas 1(800)766-9012	Missouri 1(800)392-2161	North Carolina 1(800)662-7030	South Dakota 1(800)452-7691	Wisconsin 1(800)362-3002
Delaware 1(800)372-2022	Kentucky 1(800)635-2570	Montana 1(800)362-8312	North Dakota 1(800)755-2604	Tennessee 1(800)669-1851	Wyoming 1(800)251-1269
Florida 1(850)488-3560	Louisiana 1(888)342-6207 in-state calls only		Northern Mariana Islands 1(808)587-3521	Texas 1(800)252-8263	

Medicare & You 2000

WHERE TO CALL FOR HELP

Health Care Financing Administration (HCFA) Regional Offices: Call about local seminars and health fairs on your Medicare health plan choices, and reporting a complaint.

If you live in:	The Regional Office is in:	The phone number is:
Connecticut, Maine, Massachusetts, New Hampshire, Rhode Island, Vermont	Boston	1(617)565-1232
New Jersey, New York, Puerto Rico, Virgin Islands	New York	1(212)264-3657
Delaware, Maryland, Pennsylvania, Virginia, Washington D.C., West Virginia	Philadelphia	1(215)861-4226
Alabama, Florida, Georgia, Kentucky, Mississippi, North Carolina, South Carolina, Tennessee	Atlanta	1(404)562-7500
Illinois, Indiana, Michigan, Minnesota, Ohio, Wisconsin	Chicago	1(312)353-7180
Arkansas, Louisiana, New Mexico, Oklahoma, Texas	Dallas	1(214)767-6401
Iowa, Kansas, Missouri, Nebraska	Kansas City	1(816)426-2866
Colorado, Montana, North Dakota, South Dakota, Utah, Wyoming	Denver	1(303)844-4024
American Samoa, Arizona, California, Guam, Hawaii, Nevada, Northern Mariana Islands	San Francisco	1(415)744-3602
Alaska, Idaho, Oregon, Washington	Seattle	1(206)615-2354

Medicare & You 2000

AREA AGENCIES ON AGING
Responsible for Coordinating Services for Older Persons

ALABAMA
1-800-243-5463

ALASKA
1-907-269-3680

AMERICAN SAMOA
1-684-633-1252

ARIZONA
1-602-542-4446

ARKANSAS
1-501-682-2441

CALIFORNIA
1-916-322-5290

COLORADO
1-303-620-4147

CONNECTICUT
1-800-443-9946

DELAWARE
1-800-223-9074

DISTRICT OF COLUMBIA
1-202-724-5622

FLORIDA
1-803-253-6177

GEORGIA
1-605-773-3656

GUAM
011-671-475-0263

HAWAII
1-512-424-684

IDAHO
1-801-538-3910

ILLINOIS
1-802-241-2400

INDIANA
1-804-662-9333

IOWA
1-515-281-5187

KANSAS
1-913-296-4986

KENTUCKY
1-502-564-6930

LOUISIANA
1-504-342-7100

MAINE
1-207-624-5335

MARYLAND
1-800-243-3425

MASSACHUSSETTS
1-617-727-7750

MICHIGAN
1-517-373-8230

MINNESOTA
1-800-882-6262

MISSISSIPPI
1-601-359-4929

MISSOURI
1-850-414-2000

MONTANA
1-404-657-5258

NEBRASKA
1-615-741-2056

NEVADA
1-808-586-0100

NEW HAMPSHIRE
1-208-334-2423

NEW JERSEY
1-217-785-3356

NEW MEXICO
1-317-232-7020

NEW YORK
1-800-342-9871

NORTH CAROLINA
1-919-733-3983

NORTH DAKOTA
1-800-755-8521

N. MARIANA ISLES
1-607-234-6011

OHIO
1-614-466-5500

OKLAHOMA
1-405-521-2327

OREGON
1-800-232-3020

PENNSYLVANIA
1-717-783-1550

PUERTO RICO
1-787-721-5710

RHODE ISLAND
1-401-222-2858

SOUTH CAROLINA
1-573-751-3082

SOUTH DAKOTA
1-406-444-7781

TENNESSEE
1-402-471-2306

TEXAS
1-702-486-3545

UTAH
1-603-271-4680

VERMONT
1-609-588-3139

VIRGIN ISLANDS
1-809-692-5950

VIRGINIA
1-505-837-7640

WASHINGTON
1-360-586-8753

WEST VIRGINIA
1-304-558-3317

WISCONSIN
1-608-266-2536

WYOMING
1-307-777-7986

Medicare Helpline   All States   **1-800-MEDICARE**
Call about: **TTY: 1-877-486-2048**
    TTY/TDD and local phone numbers
    General Medicare Information
    Ordering Medicare Publications
    Information about Health Plans

Office of Inspector General   All States   **1-800-447-8477**
Call about: **TTY: 1-800-377-4950**
    Reporting Fraud and Abuse

Railroad Retirement Board   **RRB Beneficiaries Only**
Call about:
    Lost RRB Medicare card, address change ....**1-800-808-0772 (RRB)**
    Part A bills and services (Fiscal Intermediary)......................... **See Appendix**
    Part B bills and services (United Healthcare).............. **1-800-833-4455 (UHC)**

Social Security Admin.   All States   **1-800-772-1213**
                                                          TTY: 1-800-325-0778
Call about:
    Address Change
    Medicare Part A or Part B
    Lost Medicare Card

Office for Civil Rights   All States   **1-800-368-1019**
Call about:
    Discrimination

2000 CHANGES IN SOCIAL SECURITY, MEDICARE AND SUPPLEMENTAL SECURITY INCOME (SSI)

Social Security Cost-of-Living Adjustment
Beneficiaries will get a 2.4% cost-of-living increase in their monthly checks beginning in January. Also getting a 2.4% increase are pensioners of the federal government and military, disabled veterans and recipients of Supplemental Security Income (SSI).

Social Security Earnings Test
The amount of wages seniors can earn each year without losing benefits. For seniors under 65, for every $2 earned over the threshold, $1 in Social Security benefits is lost. For seniors 65-69, for every $3 earned over the threshold, $1 is withheld.

	1999	2000
Under age 65	$9,600	$10,080
Age 65-69	$15,500	$17,000
Age 70 and over	No limit	No limit
Maximum Monthly Social Security Benefit (retiring at age 65)	$1,373	$1,433
Average Monthly Social Security Benefit:		
Retired workers	$785	$804
Retired couple (both eligible)	$1,316	$1,348
Retired widow(er) alone	$757	$775
Disabled workers	$736	$754
Disabled worker and family	$1,225	$1,255
FICA Payroll Taxes: Social Security	6.20%	6.20%
Medicare	1.45%	1.45%
Self-employed	15.3%	15.3%
FICA Maximum Taxable Earnings: Social Security	$72,600	$76,200
Medicare	No Limit	No Limit
Maximum Monthly Supplemental Security Income Benefit (SSI):		
Individual	$500	$512
Couple	$751	$769

Maximum Allowable Assets for SSI	1999	2000
Individual	$ 2,000	$ 2,000
Couple	$ 3,000	$ 3,000
Medicare:		
Hospital Insurance Deductible (paid once each period of hospitalization)	$ 768	$ 776
Copayment for 61st through 90th day in hospital	$ 192/day	$ 194/day
Copayment for reserve days of hospitalization	$ 384/day	$ 388/day
Copayment for skilled nursing home care (21st through 100th day)	$ 96.00/day	$ 97.00/day
Monthly Part B Premiums deducted from Social Security check	$ 45.50	$ 45.50
Annual Part B deductible (paid once each year that Part B benefits are used)	$ 100	$ 100
Copayment for Part B services	20%	20%
Limit on the amount a physician who does not accept assignment can charge for Medicare-covered services	115% of Medicare approved amount	115% of Medicare approved amount
Monthly income limits for full QMB benefits:		
Individual	$ 707*	$ **
Couple	$ 942*	$ **
Monthly income range for 100% Part B premiums to be paid (SLMB & ALMB1):		
Individual	$ 708 - 947*	$ **
Couple	$ 943 - 1,265*	$ **
Monthly income range for a portion of Part B premiums to be paid (ALMB2):		
Individual	$ 948 - 1,222*	$ **
Couple	$ 1,266 - 1,633*	$ **

*.   These figures in effect through 3/31/00.
**   These figures not yet released. Watch <u>Aging Alert</u> for updates.

Medicare Changes in the Year 2000

As of January 1, 2000, the **Part A deductibles** that you pay for each benefit period have gone up a bit. They are as follows:

$776 for a hospital stay of 1-60 days

$194 per day for days 61-90 of a hospital stay

$388 per day for days 91-150 of a hospital stay

$97 per day for days 21-100 in a skilled nursing facility

There is **no** change in the **Part B deductible** for the year 2000.

For **Hospice Care** under **Medicare Part A**, you pay a co-payment of up to $5 for outpatient prescription drugs, and 5% of the Medicare payment amount for Respite Care. The amount you pay for Respite Care can change each year.

Under **Medicare Part B,** you pay 20% for all outpatient physical and speech therapy services, and 20% for all outpatient occupational therapy services. There is **no longer** a $1,500 limit on these services in the outpatient setting.

(QMB) The Qualified Medicare Beneficiary, the (SLMB) Specified Low-Income Beneficiary, or Qualifying Individual programs to help low income Medicare beneficiaries, may not be available in Guam, Puerto Rico, the Virgin Islands, Northern Mariana Islands, and American Samoa.

If you are retired from the Military and may be entitled to medical benefits, the correct Department of Defense phone number to call is -

1-800-538-9552.

New Medicare Health Plan Choices

Congress passed a law in 1997 that made many changes in the Medicare program. The law includes a section called Medicare + Choice, which creates new health plan options. You can continue to receive Medicare benefits as you do now, or you may be able to change to a plan that gives you at least the same (possibly more) benefits. The choice is yours.

What are the Medicare Health Plans?

Medicare now offers more health plan choices in addition to the Original Medicare Plan. However, they all may not be available in your area. These choices may include:

Original Medicare Plan

The traditional pay-per-visit arrangement that covers Part A and Part B services is now called the Original Medicare Plan. Medicare pays its share of the bill and you pay the balance of the Medicare-approved payment amount.

Original Medicare Plan with a Supplemental Insurance (Medigap) Policy

The traditional pay-per-visit arrangement that covers Part A and Part B services is now called the Original Medicare Plan. You can buy one of ten standardized Medicare supplemental insurance policies (Medigap or Medicare SELECT). These policies provide extra benefits and help cover some of your out-of-pocket costs (see page 12).

Medicare Managed Care Plan

A Medicare Managed Care Plan is a group of doctors, hospitals, and other health care providers who have agreed to provide care to Medicare beneficiaries in exchange for a fixed amount of money from Medicare every month. Medicare Managed Care Plans include Health Maintenance Organizations (HMOs), Health Maintenance Organizations with a Point of Service option (HMOs With POS), Provider Sponsored Organizations (PSOs), and Preferred Provider Organizations (PPOs).

Private Fee-for-Service Plan

A Private Fee-for-Service Plan is a private insurance plan that accepts Medicare beneficiaries. You may go to any doctor or hospital you want. The insurance plan, rather than the Medicare program, decides how much to pay for the services you receive. You may have extra benefits the Original Medicare Plan doesn't cover, but you may also face higher charges from doctors and other providers. This is not the same as the Original Medicare Plan.

1999 Guide 148

Appendix - New Medicare Health Plan Choices

New Medicare Health Plan Choices continued:

Medicare Medical Savings Account (MSA) Plan

This is a test program for approximately one percent (up to 390,000) of eligible Medicare beneficiaries. You choose a Medicare MSA health policy - a health insurance policy with a high deductible. Medicare pays the premium for the Medicare MSA health policy and makes a deposit to the Medicare MSA that you establish. You use the money deposited in your Medicare MSA to pay for medical expenses. If you don't use all the money in your Medicare MSA, next year's deposit will be added to your balance. Money can be withdrawn from a Medicare MSA for non-medical expenses, but that money will be taxed. If you enroll in a Medicare MSA Plan, you must stay in it for a full year. You can only sign up for a Medicare MSA Plan in November of each year, or during special enrollment periods. Under a Medicare MSA Plan, you may face higher charges from doctors and other providers than in the Original Medicare Plan.

Religious Fraternal Benefit Society Plans

These plans are offered by a Religious Fraternal Benefit Society for members of the society. Only members of the society may enroll. The society must meet Internal Revenue Service (IRS) and Medicare requirements for this type of organization. No other information on Religious Fraternal Benefit Society Plans is available at this time.

For more information about Medicare health plans:

- Look at a copy of the *Medicare & You 1999* handbook.
- This handbook can be found on the Internet at www.medicare.gov.
- Look at Medicare health plan comparison information on the Internet at www.medicare.gov. If you don't have a computer, your local library or senior center may be able to help you access the Medicare website.
- Ask for information on Medicare + Choice health plans available in your area by using the automated Medicare Special Information number at 1-800-318-2596.
- Call your State Health Insurance Assistance Program (see page 48).

1999 Guide

ABOUT THE AUTHOR

For more than thirteen years, Frank Singer has, in his retirement years, produced over one hundred television programs for and about seniors, acting as writer, host, interviewer and reporter. He has won numerous national and regional cable awards for his programs.

As a senior, he has experienced many illnesses, aches and pains that afflict the older generation in their aging years, as well as the joys and benefits.

His favorite slogan is from the late, celebrated actress, Helen Hayes, who said, "**To rest, is to rust.**"